BIBLICAL HISTORY
AS THE QUEST
FOR MATURITY

BIBLICAL HISTORY
AS THE QUEST
FOR MATURITY

John S. Peale

Symposium Series
Volume 15

The Edwin Mellen Press
Lewiston/Queenston

Library of Congress Cataloging-in-Publication Data

Peale, John S.
    Biblical history as the quest for maturity.

    (Symposium series / Edwin Mellen Press ; v. 15)
    Bibliography: p.
    1. Bible --History of Biblical events. 2. Christian
life--1960-   . I. Title. II. Series: Symposium
series (Edwin Mellen Press) ; v. 15.
    BS635.2.P43   1985   231.7'6   85-5067
    ISBN 0-88946-706-4 (alk. paper)

This is volume 15 in the continuing series
Symposium Series
Volume 15 ISBN 0-88946-706-4
SS Series ISBN 0-88946-989-X

The Edwin Mellen Press   The Edwin Mellen Press
Box 450   Box 67
Lewiston, New York   Queenston, Ontario
USA 14092   L0S 1L0 CANADA

Printed in the United States of America

To Lydia, who knows both
what it meant
and
what it means.

Contents

Introduction

A. The Rehearsal and the Biblical Story

The central focus of this work is on the dynamic movement of sacred history as it unfolds in the Judaic Christian Bible. After drawing an initial distinction between what are called general history and sacred history an extended rehearsal of this history will be developed. The method of this rehearsal is to characterize fundamental patterns of moments in Biblical history in which God and man related in distinctive ways. The moments will take us on a Biblical journey from the moment of creation to the moment of Jesus Christ. In the inauguration of the kingdom of Christ, the moments in Biblical history are fulfilled. The establishment of that kingdom, apparently, is yet to come.

What emerge from this rehearsal of the sacred historical story are clear applications of Biblical history to the process of becoming mature, both as Biblical Christians and mature persons as such. To rehearse sacred history is to know personally the steps and the process of becoming mature. In this sense Biblical history is viewed in this work as the quest for maturity.

B. The Distinction between General History and Sacred History

General history, as that has been recorded, is the account of what has happened in the past as events are selected and interpreted by "historians." General historians interpret what has happened by selecting certain events as important and then by understanding other happenings in the light of these events. General history explains why things happen as they have by reference to prior events or circumstances. Americans, for example, might pick out the Civil War or the assassination of President Kennedy as an important event in the light of which part of our national history may be understood. On a more personal basis, individuals understand their own lives, their own histories, by selecting certain personal events as most important.

General history is to be distinguished from sacred history. Sacred history is the story of the relationship between God and man. Sacred history is composed of a series of moments in which God has made himself known to man. In sacred history it is God who causes things to happen. Man responds to what God does. The sacred historian refers to the activity of God in the lives of men to explain why things have happened as they have.

In order to be more specific, the story of Abraham in Genesis, beginning in Chapter 12, may be considered in order to see an example of the distinction between general and sacred history. "Now the Lord said to Abram, 'Go from your country and your kindred and your father's house to the land that I will show you. And I will make of you a great nation . . . and by you all the families of the earth shall bless themselves' " (Genesis 12:1-3).[1] Immediately following, in the

1

beginning of verse 4, the Bible says, "So Abram went." God calls to Abraham, and Abraham responds at once. This is an example of sacred history in that it is God who causes things to happen in the lives of those who have faith in him.

The general historian might explain the movement of Abraham in a different way, perhaps as follows. There is evidence of a movement of peoples known as the Amorites, which occurred at about the same time that Abraham went out from his country. Terah, the father of Abraham, and his whole family were a part of this migration. Terah moved his family to Southern Canaan after first stopping at Shechem. For the general historian the cause of the movement of Abraham lay in the events and circumstances in the background of the Amoritic people. For the sacred historian the cause of the movement is the call of God.

The familiar diagram of general history being represented by a horizontal line is useful, but it would be helpful to add the feature that this line is broad, including all mankind in its path. Imagine that this line is drawn on a blackboard with chalk, the thick line being made by drawing the whole length of chalk across the board at once. In this sense general history is universal, encompassing all events which have occurred. Sacred history, on the other hand, can be represented by a thin line, within the thick path of general history, a line on which there are moments, represented by dots with vertical lines going up and joining together in God. The vertical lines represent the relationship God has with men and men have with God. In this sense, sacred history is particular, encompassing only those events in the lives of men who have a sacred historical relationship with God.

As I have defined it, the term "general history" refers to those events which are understood to be caused by prior events and circumstances. Sacred history refers to those events caused by God. The distinction thus drawn is consistent with the belief that all of general history is under God's providence. To support the belief that all general history is under the providence of God one would argue that God causes events in sacred history, which events in turn cause other events in what I call "general history." To so believe is to hold, in terms of the familiar diagram, that the thin line will get progressively thicker as more people and events are affected by God's actions in the lives of those with whom he has a sacred historical relation. In this way one could believe that God is transcendent, above and in control of events in the general history of the world. A universalist would believe that at the end of time all general history will be brought into God's kingdom. For the present let us say that the dots along the thin line represent the moments in which God is with people in sacred history, causing them to act. At the dots in the diagram God is in the world in the actions of sacred historians, and they, collectively and/or individually have the potency to affect the whole of general history.

The Biblical Christian does not deny general history. For the Biblical Christian, however, it is the movement of sacred history which, as I will argue in the Appendix in Section 10, is the primary authority. It is in sacred history that man has a relationship with God, and it is in sacred history that God makes himself known to man and causes things to happen in the world. It is a rehearsal of the moments in the sacred historical story that is given in the Bible. What the Bible is about primarily is man's sacred historical relationship with God.

To say this does not imply that there is no general history, nor is it to suggest that whatever the general history is matters little or none at all. The general historian is an empiricist. He is interested in what "really happened" in the past. How he knows, or at least believes, that what happened is known to have happened is on the basis of certain specific sorts of empirical evidence, that is, on actual records or artifacts. To be sure, what the general historian believes is relevant in a sense, for he selects certain events from among the happenings he has observed and interprets other happenings in the light of these events.

For such an empirically minded historian the specific belief in God is irrelevant, for there are no empirical records or artifacts which would show God to this historian. In his effort to explain why things have happened as they have, the general historian would count as relevant that others believed in God, but the belief in God for the historian is not relevant to his work as a historian.

For the sacred historian, or the man of faith, the situation with respect to history is radically different. What the sacred historian wants to know is how God is acting in history, his own history and in the general history of the world. What is God causing to happen? What is the character of the relationship which the historian himself, or the Church, or movements in the world have with God? His knowledge of what really has happened and is happening is what God is doing in his world and how people are responding to such divine activity.

C. Maturity

In Biblical Christian language I will say that the mature person is one who takes God in Christ to be Lord of his life. To see what this means one can immerse oneself in the moments of the sacred historical story, for example, the moment in the garden, the Abrahamic moment, the moment of the exodus, the Isaiah moment, the fall of Jerusalem moment, the moment of Jesus the Christ, the moment when the Church was born. One can see himself and his life and the life of the Church and the world in which he is involved in the rehearsal of the moments of sacred history. The moments may be viewed as seasons of the spirit. It becomes clear what it is to be led by God through spiritual seasons of faithfulness, times of testing, success and unity, unfaithfulness, and moments of hope even in perilous times.

In all of these a person sees the fully developed or mature Christian life, which is lived under the providence of God through all these moments. One will see that all the moments are relived and fulfilled in the moment of Jesus the Christ. In him all the ways that God and man have related are relived and all the promises of God to man are fulfilled, but the final establishment of these promises is yet to come. All this is to be seen in the rehearsal of the seasons of the spirit.

In all of these a person can also learn what it is to have God in Christ as Lord of his life. He can learn this as he compares himself positively and negatively to the Biblical characters in the moments in the rehearsal. He can learn this as he attends to the movement of sacred history from moment to moment, to the repetitions and patterns represented therein.

He can learn this as he understands that God is leading him through all the seasons of the spirit from the beginning point of faith to the fulfillment of his purposes at the end of time. In leading him, in saving him even from himself, God is working out his purposes in the general history of the world. To react faithfully to this belief in all the varying circumstances of life as reflected in the rehearsal of the sacred historical moments is what it means to take God in Christ as Lord.

In the moments of the rehearsal a person also sees what it is to be personally mature as such. Thus he will know an Abrahamic maturity, a maturity of freedom in his exodus moment of the spirit, a maturity of bondage in his wilderness and law moments, a Davidic maturity and, finally, and in culmination, he will know the maturity of Jesus the Christ.

What is my definition of maturity? Maturity is often distinguished from "maturation" which refers to processes of various sorts which lead to or culminate in a state of the person designated by the term "maturity".[2] It is said to be a commendable adult state of one of three basic forms: intellectual, emotional and social.[3]

There is a state of intellectual maturity. This is called "practical wisdom," and it includes the making of practical judgments which affect life. For example, it includes moral judgments as to what is standard or acceptable within a certain social milieu. It includes ethical and value judgments as to what is right or obligatory or good under specified action guiding principles. I will argue that such intellectual maturity is presupposed by other senses of maturity.

There is also a state of emotional maturity. This often is identified with a steadiness of emotions, or feelings, or at least a steadiness in the behavioral manifestations of these emotions or feelings. The mature person, like all others, can and does have radical changes of feeling in both intensity and duration, but nonetheless there is a steadiness to his life, especially to his behavior, even so. For there to be such a steadiness of behavior, there is required a factor in the explanation of behavior distinct from the feelings themselves, and that, conveniently enough, may be said to be the factor of practically-wise judgments. Unlike feelings and emotions, practical judgments, based as they are on some reasons, are potentially permanent and neutral with respect to intensity. So the emotionally mature man is one whose faculty of practical wisdom is not interrupted by the reality of rapidly fluctuating feelings or emotions.

Third among the given forms of maturity is social maturity, referring most often to behavior which is socially acceptable or standard in a given social milieu. A socially mature person is one who can discern what social standards or acceptable patterns of behavior are within a given social context. In this discernment is the exercise of practical wisdom or intellectual maturity. Unless there is some good reason for acting otherwise, the socially mature individual will act in accordance with these socially acceptable standards of behavior. Such good reasons would include, for example, ethical principles. Such ethical standards based on principle might not, in a given social milieu, conform to standard or acceptable behavior within the same cultural context. Within a given social milieu a socially mature person may refuse to follow socially acceptable standards because he regards them in violation of ethical principles. Thus his social maturity presupposes his practical wisdom.

So there are three forms of the commendable state of maturity: intellectual, emotional and social. In varying senses, as I have shown, the emotional and social maturity each presuppose the intellectual.

My own working definition of the mature person is as follows: it is a commendable state of the adult person in which there is a dynamic between developed senses of both independence and self-sufficiency on the one hand and dependence and, for want of a better term, self-insufficiency on the other hand.

First of all, the mature person is one who has a sense of his own independence. He is a free autonomous agent, and in this is his independence. More than that, however, he is sufficient unto himself. He can stand on his own, making his own decisions, on the basis of his own reasons, adjusting himself to his own mix of feelings. He has the will power to act on his own, and he can accept and live comfortably with the consequences of his actions without having to receive the commendation of support or criticism of any other person. In this sense the mature person leans on nothing but himself. In this he is self-sufficient. On the one side he is both independent and self-sufficient.

But there is the other side of this concept of the mature person. He is also dependent. As independent he is a free autonomous person. So he can freely become dependent, choosing to enter into those webs of dependencies found in his natural associations, say with family, friends or partners. He freely and gladly accepts the fact that he is dependent on others for so much of his life. So much of what is valuable he finds as he shares life with others, as he is concerned for others, as he gives himself for the betterment of others, and as he receives similarly from them. In these senses it is only the dependent person that can find true love with others and also true friendship. One has to be dependent in order to achieve the sort of closeness required by true love or friendship.

Just as self-sufficiency carries us one step beyond independence so there is a step beyond dependence, which I will call self-insufficiency. This is an absolute dependence, dependency to the degree that the independent self has been lost or surrendered to that on which one is dependent. To be self-insufficient is to have lost one's self or at least any reliance thereon.

So the mature person is one both independent and self-sufficient yet also dependent on other people and circumstances. At times he may be self-insufficient. The mature life, I think, would be one in which there is a dynamic between independence and dependence and between their correlates, self-sufficiency and self-insufficiency. When circumstances are appropriate the mature person will be able to stand alone, having within himself all that is necessary to do just that. On the other hand he can and does live in his web of dependencies. It is an act of mature practical wisdom to judge when to be dependent and self-insufficient and when to be independent and self-sufficient.

The definition of the mature person in terms of this dynamic of dependence and independence is basic to and logically prior to other characterizations we are given of the mature person. As noted above a person is intellectually mature in that he possesses what is called practical wisdom. This may mean that he has "clear, objective, and undistorted views" of both himself and his world, or it may mean that a mature person knows what he wants of life, what he wants to do or what he believes is right. He has a sense of purpose. He can accept others for what they are, and he is free to open himself to others, not having that reserve that comes from personal insecurity.

If a person is emotionally mature he is able to keep his head even in times of difficult emotional strain, to keep a balanced view. Again a person is socially mature insofar as a person acts in a way that is acceptable within the given social milieu, except for good reasons to act otherwise.

But these characterizations are all based on the two-fold dynamic between independence and dependence. To give any one of these three characterizations of the state of maturity is just to say that a mature person can step out of any situation alone and independently and view it from a sense of detachment, at least for a time. It is the mature person who independently knows himself, who is free to open himself to and for others, even in certain circumstances to let himself go and be dependent, even absolutely so, on them.

A word about my use of pronouns is in order at the outset of this rehearsal. When I say "we," "us," or "our" I refer to the Biblical Christian or to the mature person as such. This work is a proposal in thought. It will help us to take an inside point of view, as if we ourselves are Biblical Christians or as if we ourselves are questing for maturity. Within this work as a whole I will use the singular personal pronoun "I" to indicate precisely the points I as the author want to make or the conclusions I wish to show.

2

The Beginning Moments

A. Creation

"In the beginning God created the heavens and the earth" (Genesis 1:1). This first verse of the Bible speaks of the activity of God, the act of creation of the world. The accounts of creation are two, and they are given in the first two chapters of the book of Genesis, the first in Genesis 1:1—2:4a, and the second in Genesis 2:4b—2:25.[1]

This first moment in the sacred historical story is the moment in which God and man begin to relate as creator and creature. The beginning for the Biblical Christian is the starting point of faith, which, according to the sacred historical way of thinking, begins with the activity of God. In the beginning God creates a relationship with man, and out of nothing but himself and his love he creates all the conditions for our having a sacred historical relationship with him, all the conditions for our acknowledgement of him as Lord.

In the first of the creation accounts in Genesis we read how he creates the heavens and the earth (Genesis 1:1), the light of day and the dark of night (Genesis 1:5). He brings dry land out of the water (Genesis 1:9), and he makes the earth as we know it, the vegetation and plants (Genesis 1:11). He brings "forth swarms of living creatures" of all kinds, in the air (Genesis 1:20), in the sea (Genesis 1:21) and on the earth (Genesis 1:24-25). Then God said, "Let us make man in our image, after our likeness; and let them have dominion over . . . (all other creatures). So God created man in his own image, in the image of God he created him" (Genesis 1:26-27).

In the second account of the creation accounts we read how "the Lord God formed man of dust from the ground, and breathed into his nostrils the breath of life; and man became a living being" (Genesis 2:7). And the Lord God took care of man, creating all the conditions for him to live as he was meant to live. He planted a garden, and he put man in it, this man who is the dust of the ground in which God breathed the breath of life. "And God saw everything that he had made, and behold, it was very good" (Genesis 1:31).

The beginning moment of creation is the moment when God creates us and our whole world, and he creates us in his own image to be a creature of his. We have a sacred historical relationship with him because he has begun his creative activity.

B. In the Garden (before the Fall)

Our sacred history begins, therefore, with an act of the very God who creates us. We are creatures of God who created us. It is for us to respond to what God has done for us.

What he has done for us is to place us in a garden (See Genesis 2:8-9). In our sacred history, that is, our relationship with God, the garden means that spiritual state in which we have unbroken communion with him and the same with each other. In its own cryptic way the Bible expresses the fact of our communion with each other as follows: "And the man and his wife were both naked, and were not ashamed" (Genesis 2:25). We may take this symbolically to mean that in the beginning point of our faith we have nothing to hide from one another.

In the garden, where God saw that everything was good, we may say that man was dominated by a consciousness of God, man does what God commands, and man does not do what God forbids. God had said, "You may freely eat of every tree of the garden, but of the tree of the knowledge of good and evil you shall not eat, for in the day that you eat of it you shall die" (Genesis 2:17).

C. The Fall and Expulsion

In our sacred historical relationship with God it is we who fall, we who break the bonds of perfect communion which have been established by God in his creative activity. We choose things other than God to be Lord of our histories, of our personal lives.

In the Biblical account this act of our rebellion is told to us in the form of the story of the serpent and the woman in Genesis 3. The serpent is not bad, for God had created everything, including the serpent, and behold, it was good.

The serpent first quotes God, which is not bad: "Did God say, 'You shall not eat of any tree of the garden'?" (Genesis 3:1). Eve tells the serpent what God did say. Then the serpent contradicts what God had said, which still is not evil. He stated what he believed to be factual. "You will not die," he said, "for God knows that when you eat of it your eyes will be opened, and you will be like God, knowing good and evil" (Genesis 3:4-5).

What follows is what is evil. What follows is the fall. What follows is our choice to break the bond of communion which God has established for us. What follows is a breakdown of the Lordship of Christ in our lives. It is a good idea to look very specifically at what tempted the woman to fall away from what God had set for her.

First, she saw that the fruit of the tree of the knowledge of good and evil was good for food (Genesis 3:6). She wanted what was good for food for herself. She went against one of the injunctions Jesus was later to give: Be not anxious about what you shall eat or drink or what you shall wear, but seek first the kingdom of God (Matthew 6:25 and 33). The concern of the woman, as with us all, is what is good for our own well being.

Next, the woman saw that the tree was a "delight to the eyes" (Genesis 3:6). She was sensitive to what was beautiful and delightful to the senses. How often it is that such delights lead us astray.

Thirdly, the woman saw "that the tree was to be desired to make one wise" (Genesis 3:6). The woman wanted to become wise, and how often it is that in desiring to be wise in ourselves we are failing to acknowledge the Lordship of God in our lives. None of these temptations of the woman is in itself bad. None in itself disrupts the sacred historical relationship we have with Almighty God.

What the serpent said to Eve is that in eating of the fruit of the tree her eyes would be opened, and she would "be like God, knowing good and evil" for herself. This desire to be like God is what breaks the relationship of unbroken communion that God has established for us and between us. We want to be gods ourselves. We want to know good and evil for ourselves. We want to direct ourselves to the ends that we think are right for us. We want what is good for food for us. We want what delights our senses. We want more and more and more of delights, sensory and sensual. We want to be wise and knowledgeable in and for ourselves.

What we have here in the fall is the birth of self-consciousness, which self-consciousness is fed constantly by these desires and temptations. And the growth of this self-consciousness has the effect in us of blotting out the consciousness of God.

So we no longer have God as the Lord of our histories, for we have elevated ourselves to the rank of Lords over our own lives. Our eyes are opened and we know that we are naked, and we sew fig leaves together to make aprons for ourselves, sometimes very fashionable aprons, so that we can hide ourselves from each other (Genesis 3:7). We hide from God when we hear "the sound of the Lord God walking in the cool of the day" (Genesis 3:8).

By our act of choosing to fall away from what God has established for us and from what God has called us to do and be, we have created the problem for which the rest of the Biblical story is the answer.

God expels us from the garden, which symbolizes the fact that the relationship of communion with God has been broken. God expels us, lest we, who are now little gods in and for ourselves, reach out and "take also of the tree of life, and eat, and live for ever" (Genesis 3:22).

We live and struggle under the burden of God's word upon us. The word for the woman is that there shall be pain in childbearing and subservience to a husband (Genesis 3:16), and for the man that there will be unending toil amid "thorns and thistles" and the eating of bread with sweat on the face (Genesis 3:18, 19). All this is our burden until we "return to the ground, for out of it you were taken; you are dust, and to dust you shall return" (Genesis 3:19).

In our sacred historical story, our relationship with God, in which God was Lord of our history, has been broken. The rest of the Biblical story is the story of the recovery of this relationship with God, a recovery of the Lordship of God in Christ in our lives.

D. The Problem of Spiritual and Moral Autonomy

This problem emerges out of our rehearsal, most directly out of the moment of the fall, in which moment there is the birth of self-consciousness.

Like the woman in the garden the Biblical Christian and the mature person want to be like God, knowing good and evil for themsleves. They want to be autonomous agents, spiritually in their relation to God, and morally in their deliberation as to what they ought or ought not to do. For his part the Biblical Christian believes that God made him this way by creating him, by placing him in a garden, by giving him his world. God set down restrictions, to be sure. He told man not to eat of the fruit of the tree of the knowledge of good and evil. He did not, however, create man so that he had no choice in the matter. So man stands before his God as a free agent.

It seems that man may do or not do what God has laid out for him. At the least he is free not to do it. He is free to do what is wrong; he is free to break the law given to him by his God. The question for the Biblical Christian is what it is for God in Christ to be Lord. At the beginning moment the Biblical Christian can say this: God has given him his world. He has not done this because of any special merit of his; he has done it out of his love for man. The most the Biblical Christian can do is to love him in return. In the language of the New Testament, what man may do is to love him with his whole being, his whole heart, mind, soul, and strength. Thus is the "Great Commandment."

If the Biblical Christian follows this commandment, he will be taking God to be the one and only authority in his life, in all that he feels, thinks and does as a consequence of his emotions and thoughts. Thus he will be dominated by a consciousness of God, as were the man and the woman in the garden before the fall. As such he will lose self-consciousness and all the temptations known to the woman, which came with its birth.

But then it will follow that man will not be the free autonomous agent he thinks that God has made him to be. He will not be spiritually free in himself to make decisions affecting himself, nor will he be morally free, able to decide to do what God has commanded him not to do.

The free exercise of personal traits, emotions, thoughts, volitions are required for him to be an autonomous spiritual and moral agent. For man before God there is the freedom, the right, even the obligation to exercise all the personal powers which have been given him.

The image of ourselves as men, as free spiritual agents, is important. It is one of man's ground floor beliefs. The same may be said for the sense of being moral agents. Man believes that he has a freedom, an autonomy to make moral decisions affecting his own life. Some have said that this autonomy is the foundation, the precondition of morality itself.

In short, the problem is this: if God who gave man his spiritual and moral autonomy is to be Lord, then man has to sacrifice the very autonomy God has given him. The rehearsal so far has taught that this problem, phrased differently, also applies to the mature person as such. Man has spiritual and moral autonomy, yet in being a Biblical Christian or in being mature, man has to give it up. How can this be explained?

The problem of spiritual and moral autonomy is exemplified in one of the strongest statements of what the Biblical Christian is to do and be as a Biblical Christian, namely in what is called the "Sermon on the Mount" (Matthew 5—7). Those who are blessed are said to be those who are "poor in spirit," who are "merciful," who are "pure in heart," who are "peacemakers," "who are persecuted for righteousness sake" (Matthew 5:8-10). Such descriptions as these are those of people who do not have strong senses of themselves, certainly not of themselves as people valuing their sense of being free spiritual and moral autonomous agents. It may be said that such descriptions are of people who love God with their whole being, who have God in Christ as their Lord. For these people there is the "kingdom of heaven," "comfort," "inheritance of the earth," "satisfaction," "mercy," "the sight of God," and the name of "sons of God" (Matthew 5:3-10). This is the message of what we call the "beatitudes."

It is said that man cannot serve both God and mammon (Matthew 6:24). He cannot serve both God and his own spiritual, moral, and autonomous self. So he is not to think of himself, not to be anxious about his life, his food, as was the woman in the garden, his drink, or his clothes. He is not to protect and nourish his free spiritual and moral dignity and individuality. Rather, the Biblical Christian is to "seek first his kingdom and his righteousness" (Matthew 6:33). He is to be dominated by consciousness of God. He is to lose the sense of himself.

Since this sense of ourselves is so important to us, and since the image of ourselves as free autonomous agents is such a basic conception for morality and spirituality, it becomes clear that the loss of this autonomy is a problem. How can a view of Biblical Christianity which holds that this autonomy has to be sacrificed be defended? A critical discussion of the problem and its resolution will be given in Section 10.

E. The Noah Movement

Noah was a good and righteous man, who lived among all the wickedness and evil that men had brought upon themselves. "The Lord saw that the wickedness of man was great in the earth" (Genesis 6:5). "And the Lord was sorry that he had made man upon the earth, and it grieved him to his heart" (Genesis 6:16). What God wanted to do was to blot out man who had so badly fallen away. But Noah had "found favor in the eyes of the Lord" (Genesis 6:8). "God remembered Noah" (Genesis 8:1).

What God did was to send a flood to wash the world clean of all sin and wickedness. From such cleansing he saved Noah and his family and "seven pairs of all clean animals" (Genesis 7:2) all of whom waited out the flood in the ark. In this saving by cleansing God is separating out his people from all other peoples on the earth.

When the flood was over, Noah built an altar to the Lord and offered burnt offerings upon the altar (Genesis 8:20). And when the Lord smelled the pleasing odor, the Lord said in his heart, "I will never again curse the ground because of man, for the imagination of man's heart is evil from his youth; neither will I ever again destroy every living creature as I have done" (Genesis 8:21). And God blessed Noah (Genesis 9:1), and God established his covenant with Noah (Genesis 9:8-12).

But Noah, who was the first tiller of the soil (Genesis 9:20), was also like all of us in that he too had his weaknesses and temptations. He "drank of the wine, and became drunk, and lay uncovered in his tent" (Genesis 9:21). His sons, Shem and Japeth, covered his nakedness with their faces turned, so they could not see their father in his condition (Genesis 9:23).

Noah blessed them for what they had done. As God had perceived, Noah was a good man, but also he was human. Like ours the imagination of his heart was evil from his youth. So he fell short in faithfulness, succumbing to the temptation to drink. We too know what it is to succumb to this temptation. When in our weakness we do give in to temptation, as did the woman in the garden, God in Christ is no longer Lord of our lives.

In summary, "First, Noah was singled out of the many inhabitants of the earth because of his character and his relationship with God. He had to work *alone* to *build an ark* to house his family and each species of the earth. Second, God was inspired to carry out his threat, because of the promise of a *new beginning* after his judgment on the wickedness, violence, and corruption and after that had been eliminated from the earth. Thus a *cleansing* effect was necessitated justifying the destruction by flooding. Third, the Lord expressed *sorrow* for destroying the earth and consequently made a covenant with Noah promising never to destroy the earth again by a flood."[2]

F. Universalism and the Problem of "The Others"

In the Noah moment in the rehearsal of the sacred historical story the problem of "the others" is raised for the first time. God called Noah and his family and two of every kind of living thing to separate themselves out by going into the ark. During the flood God washed the world clean. He blotted out men who had fallen away. These persons blotted out I will call "the others."

"The others" are clearly a mixed lot. I will propose a complex definition of this mixed class of persons. Accordingly, and with attention to the logical possibilities, "the others" is a class of persons including the following subclasses: (1) those who have not heard God's word; (2) those who have heard but who have chosen otherwise, the stubbornly unrepentent; (3) those who are too ignorant to choose and who are unable to overcome their ignorance, the invincibly ignorant; (4) those who are sincere practitioners of religious traditions other than Christianity; (5) those who simply do not care.

That there are others is consistent with the theological doctrine of election, the view that God elected a people, among other peoples, made a special covenantal relationship with the elect, and excluded others from that to which the elect were elected. If there are those excluded by God, perhaps this represents a sixth class, (6) those whom God himself has denied or excluded.

By universalism I will understand the view that in the end of time under the providence of God all will be saved. If universalism is true, there is no final problem of "the others"; if false, there is. The problem is whether or not universalism, as so defined, is true. In Section 10 a view on this doctrine will be offered.

There are universalistic passages in the Bible. This will be evident in the unfolding of the sacred historical story (See Genesis 12:3). There will be obvious universalistic implications in Second Isaiah. There are also such in the New Testament (See Colossians 3:11; Second Peter 3:8-10). These and other passages will be discussed when I give my solution to this problem in Section 10, the Appendix.

G. The Beginnings of the Quest for Maturity

The natural condition of man can be considered independently of the question of his relation to God. It can be discussed on its own right in terms of personal maturity. The state of man "in the beginning" is not that he is or needs to become "mature." For him in his primitive state the world simply is a given, as also is the social web of personal relations. Both are givens in which he finds himself. This world and these relationships are created for man, he knows not how. Man has been given his life in the world and the conditions in which to live it.

In the beginning man has a sense of unbroken communion with others in a web of relationships wherein he finds himself. In the beginning persons are fathers or mothers, sons and daughters, brothers and sisters. They live and move and have their being in a kinship system in which they find themselves. I will say that the community is a true community in the beginning insofar as man functions in his proper station in life. He is given all he needs to live in this true community. To be sure he is a creature, for his life has been created. He does not, however, stand apart from this community in which he finds himself. He is not dependent on it, but rather he is an integral part of it.

In the beginning there are restrictions placed upon man, upon his activity in the community. These are communal or social restrictions placed upon him entirely because of the kinship system in which he finds himself. There is a network of duties and responsibilities he is supposed to observe. These are entirely due to his position as a family member, friend or enemy, or whatever. The restrictions themselves are a given for him. He does not have them because he freely and "maturely" has decided that he has and ought to follow these duties and responsibilities. He has found himself at a certain place in the kinship system, thus his restrictions.

The natural man, as opposed to the sacred historian or man of faith, also has certain temptations to which he is awakened, temptations all having to do with himself. Such temptations present themselves in the course of his life and indeed in all our lives in the world. The occasions themselves may be construed as wily and crafty "serpents." These tricky agents talk with us, doubting openly that we need to adhere to the restrictions imposed on us in our kinship systems.

In the first instance we see some things that are good for us and some things that are not. For example we see what is good for food for us. We want what is good for food for us. We become quite concerned with what is for our own well-being. We think egoistically. Secondly, we are concerned with what appeals to our sense, what delights us sensorily and sensually. We all find we like such delights and the consequent pleasures which come from receiving them. We want more and more of them and various kinds and intermixings of them. In our own privacy we wallow in them and in ourselves we dwell on them and secretly crave them. Our drive for pleasure is not yet curtailed or restricted by self-imposed and realistic limits. The pleasure principle is not yet regulated by the reality principle. In this "state of nature" we are desire-driven creatures out to get what we want for ourselves.

We also are tempted by the desire to be wise in ourselves, for such practical wisdom will help us get what we want better and more efficiently. We want to be smart, smarter than the other person, smart enough to know what is good for us. If we are smart, we reason that we can gain a greater amount and a more sensitive mixture of the delights and pleasures we crave.

The final temptation is to choose to direct ourselves for ourselves. We want to be freed from the over-arching direction of the true community in which we have found ourselves. There creeps into our consciousness the "I" or the direct awareness of ourselves, of these temptations for ourselves, and we succumb to these temptations in what may be called a "fall." In the beginning we were in paradise, in that everything we needed for our lives was given us through the true community of which we were a part. This original was simply a given fact of our experience.

But we are no longer in paradise after the communion is broken. This "fall" of ours has set up a problem for which the quest for maturity is an, if not the, answer. In our "fall" we have become conscious of ourselves, and we now know that we need to develop this self. We have our desires for what delights us and gives us pleasure for ourselves, but we see the need for tempering our drive for pleasure with a little reality, a little common sense. We see that to maximize our sensory and sensual delights we need a certain steadiness. We do not want emotional highs to be followed by lows. A steadiness is desirable. At the very least we see the need for a reflection of this emotional steadiness in our behavior.

In our quest for maturity we learn that we need a practical wisdom to discern what is best for our own lives and for our relationships with others. Not only do we want to know what is good for food for our own nourishment, but we want to know what is best for us in every area of our lives. We need to be able to make practically wise judgments for our lives, judgments about what is prudent or moral or ethical, judgments about what is virtuous or of value to ourselves and to our relationships with others.

Finally we learn that we need a social maturity, an ability to act acceptably in a responsible pattern of activity with our social milieu. Deviations from such socially responsible behavior will be possible for us only when we practically judge such for what we consider good reasons. All this emphasis on ourselves, on our emotions, our practical judgments and our socially acceptable behavior is a consequence of the rupture of the true community that was in our beginning.

At this beginning moment of the quest for maturity we realize that there is a basic dynamic fluctuation from dependence to independence. In the beginning we were an integral part of a kinship system. This defined us and our relationships and our "style of life." We were not dependent on it; we were completely immersed in it. After our act of succumbing to the various temptations in our "fall" we were, in effect, separated off from our true condition, expelled as if by a greater power. We concerned ourselves with what is good for us, what delights us, what makes us wise. We became self-conscious directors of our own lives. So we became independent agents for ourselves. In our independence, however, we come to know moments of dependence in, for example, our relationship in the still existing kinship system. We have come to realize the dependence only after we became self-conscious and, thereby in a sense, independent.

In our quest for maturity there will be Noah moments for us. There will be moments in which we take account of our lives and our relationships and judge that we have been acting prudently and morally and rightly, that we have sought things of value and developed virtuous habits in ourselves. In short we will judge that we are righteous. We would think that something of the true community in which we found ourselves in the beginning has been recovered at least in our family. We do stand independent of this community though, at least in the sense that we make judgments about it.

In our independence we also make judgments about the state of society as a whole. We would be able to have a vision of the society, and we would judge that it had fallen away from the spirit of the true community man had in the beginning. We would make practically wise judgments about the immature attitudes and behavior of our fellow human beings outside our family. We would be able to discern a social malaise. At the least we could see the ruinous character of lives spent through following the temptations of the moment. We could see that people around us had not achieved an emotional maturity. In their drive for egoistic satisfaction freed from the restrictions of reasonable or practical judgments, we could see that "the imagination of man's heart is evil from his youth."

The person searching for maturity would at this point have to develop the independence which he had had after his separation from the true community. Heretofore he had developed the ability to step back from his situation making practically wise judgments about it. Now more is required.

The mature man needs to become a free autonomous agent, standing on his own, making his own decisions based on his own reasons and feelings. He will have to be content with the consequences of his actions without needing or worrying about the commendation or criticism of other people. This furthering of man's independence occurs in his Noah moment.

In the Noah moments the mature person will decide to create new social conditions apart from his own culture. He will separate himself and his family and various kinds of animals. He will create the conditions for a completely new beginning. It will be a "noble experiment." It will be a society free from the corruption and predominantly egoistic behavior so common in the culture at large.

To do this the person searching for maturity needs more than independence. He needs a self-sufficiency. He needs an ability to step back from his society to judge it and also to be able to function intellectually, emotionally and socially apart from it. He needs to be able to live and work on his own. He needs to be self-sufficient. His condemnation of the general culture will not set well with his contemporaries who are the object of this harsh judgment. We will have to work alone to build the conditions for developing the new society he sees in his vision. He will be ridiculed, or at least, misunderstood. Because of the promise of a new beginning he will, however, persevere.

There will come the time of the cleansing of the world, or at least Noah's world, so that the new beginning can be realized. For a time it will be realized. After a time, however, the ineffectiveness of such new beginnings in the quest for maturity will be realized instead. There is more to maturity than independence and self-sufficiency. Although this is the central mark of the Noah moment in the mature life, it is also the mark of failure. Man, even in his quest for maturity, finds that he cannot remain standing alone. He must choose to enter and be sustained by the new community which develops after the period of cleansing.

In the new and emerging community of which he is a part he will find that the evil which had been cleansed away reappears. Again men seek, as they did in their "fall," to think and behave egoistically. We all seem to have this penchant which violates our practical judgments, which interrupts our emotional and social steadiness. Often we take too much of what we think is a good thing, even getting "drunk" and being "naked" and destroying our familial relationships. The close familial bonds in the true community which we have recovered will again be ruptured. Gradually we come to the realization that the evil is actually in our own hearts and not in the world. As in the beginning of our quest for maturity we see that the evil lies in our act of succumbing to temptations as man did in his beginning moments. The evil in man's heart which runs counter to the realization of true community is the egoistic thinking which distorts wise practical judgments, which renders us all emotionally and socially immature.

So even in the independence and self-sufficiency of a Noah moment, a person searching for maturity is lacking. The quest is not to be realized in the Noah moment. In spite of the self-sufficiency and the consequent practically wise judgments, man again turns to his evil ways. Even the good and righteous man will fall into temptation. The person searching for maturity will be sorry that such a separation and a new beginning has occurred. He will make an agreement with all those in the new community that never again will they separate themselves from the rest of mankind. They are sorry that that was done. A separation of men from men and a cleansing of the world from evil is not the answer.

3

The Moment of Abraham

A. The Abrahamic Journey

In the story of Abraham, which is found in Genesis 12—23, we learn much about what it is to have God in Christ as Lord of our histories. Abraham was a man who remained faithful even in the time of his greatest and most difficult trials. As Paul says, "Abraham believed God, and it was reckoned to him as righteousness" (Romans 4:3). Yet, as we shall see, Abraham was not always Abrahamic.

The story begins in Genesis 12:1-4. In that passage is the first point about Lordship. God calls Abraham to go from his country and his kindred and his father's house to "a land that I will show you" (Genesis 12:1). Immediately after God's call the Bible says, "So Abram went."

With Abraham, then, the first point is this: when God calls, Abraham goes. There is no hesitation or qualification. Following the call of God, Abraham responds, immediately. The lesson for us is plain: to have God in Christ as our Lord we have to live in a state of readiness to follow the call of God whenever that comes. We are not told that we are not to make plans, to secure our futures, to increase our possessions, to be concerned with our comforts and our welfare. To do these things is not ruled out. At the same time, however, we are to be prepared to take risks, to give up our possessions, to change our plans. We are to live on the threshold of readiness to follow the call of God, whenever or however that call comes to us.

The question of how we know that it is God who is calling us when we are called will be deferred until after consideration of the three lessons we learn from the Abrahamic story.

Secondly, Abraham is called by God to go "to the land that I will show you." The remainder of God's call in Genesis 12:1-3 is in the future tense. The point is that Abraham is ready and willing to go out from everything he is familiar with, his country, his kindred and his father's house, into a future he knows not what. All he has is his faith that God will show him the land, and that there will be a nation made of him, by which "all the families of the earth shall bless themselves" (Genesis 12:3).

What this means is that God is calling Abraham, just as God sometimes calls us, to go into an uncertain future. We know of our penchant for making plans or for securing our futures. We do these things, but they must be fragile. We must be ready to take the risk and face the anxiety that stepping into an unknown future involves. If God is Lord of our histories, if he is authoritative in our lives, then we are to be dependent on him and him only. If he calls us into a future we cannot foresee, we must believe in what he promises, and we must be prepared to follow, no matter what.

The first point is hard to follow, and the second is even harder. The third is the most demanding of all. This point is found in Genesis 22, in the story of God testing Abraham, by calling on him to sacrifice his son, Isaac.

Who was Isaac? First, he was the son of Abraham, and fathers love their sons. God is calling on Abraham to sacrifice his son, his only son, Isaac, whom he loves, "and go to the land of Moriah, and offer him there as a burnt offering upon one of the mountains of which I shall tell you" (Genesis 22:2).

But Isaac was more than just the son whom the father, Abraham, loved. Isaac also was the gift of God to Abraham. In Genesis 18 the Lord appears to Abraham "by the oaks of Mamre as he sat by the door of his tent" (Genesis 18:1). He said that Sarah, Abraham's wife, would have a son. Sarah laughed. She laughed because she was beyond her child-bearing age. She laughed because she knew that she could not bear a child.

But she did. Isaac, therefore, was a gift given by God, a gift given by a power greater than that of Abraham and Sarah. Now God was calling on Abraham to sacrifice that gift. This was more than Abraham could understand.

But Isaac was not only a beloved son and a gift. Indeed he represented all that Abraham hoped for as a man of faith. God was to make a great nation of Abraham. And how would this be done, but through Abraham's son, and his son's sons, and through the multiplication of descendants? So God was calling on Abraham to sacrifice all the hopes that God himself had given to Abraham. How could Abraham understand this?

Abraham was a man of faith, who had been called by God. In response to that call Abraham was ready immediately to go into a future he knew not what. He is ready to take the risks and to bear the uncertainty just to be faithful to God's call. Now in the 22nd chapter of Genesis God tests Abraham by calling upon him to sacrifice all his hopes, even those given as a gift to him by God.

How could Abraham understand these things? What power moved Abraham on his three-day journey with Isaac his son to the land of Moriah? On the way "Isaac said to his father Abraham, . . . 'Behold, the fire and the wood; but where is the lamb for a burnt offering?' Abraham said, 'God will provide himself the lamb for a burnt offering, my son.' So they went both of them together" (Genesis 22:7-8).

Indeed, God would provide the lamb for sacrifice. But Isaac did not know who the lamb was to be. Abraham could not explain it to him in such a way that his beloved son would keep his faith in God. (I will return to this lamb below.)

Abraham and Isaac reached their destination. An altar was built, the wood was laid in order. Then Abraham "bound Isaac his son, and laid him upon the altar, upon the wood" (Genesis 22:9). Abraham next did something in "fear and trembling." He "put forth his hand, and took the knife to slay his son" (Genesis 22:10).

What power on earth gave Abraham the strength to hold the knife in his outstretched hand, powerful and steady, ready to plunge it into Isaac his beloved son, whom God had given him?

It was at this point that Abraham had fully met his test. He had faithfully responded to God's call by being ready to go when God called him to do so, by being ready to go into a future he knew not what, by being ready to sacrifice even the greatest gift that God had given to him and Sarah, and now by being ready to sacrifice his hopes as a man of faith. He fully demonstrated that he was ready to do these things. He did not understand them. He could not explain them to Isaac or to anyone else, even to Sarah.

Abraham did not sacrifice Isaac, for at the moment in which the knife was poised God stopped Abraham. "Abraham, Abraham!" he said. "Do not lay your hand on the lad or do anything to him; for now I know that you fear God, seeing you have not withheld your son, your only son, from me" (Genesis 22:11,12).

Abraham had met his test. He "lifted up his eyes and looked and behold, behind him was a ram, caught in a thicket by his horns; and Abraham went and took the ram, and offered it up as a burnt offering instead of his son" (Genesis 22:13).

What does it mean to have God in Christ as Lord? From the story of Abraham we learn much about this. We are to be ready to follow the call of God, to live on the threshold of readiness to follow his call, no matter what our plans are. There is a fine line here between making plans, securing our futures, increasing our possessions, between all this and being ready to follow God's call as did Abraham. We may actually do all these things, but we are to be prepared to do without them. We may have those we love, those things which we treasure, which have been given to us as gifts. But we are not to be possessed by these things we have. We are not to grasp them and hold onto them too tightly.

For God to be our Lord we are to let the call of God be the one and only authority for what we are, what we feel and think, what we do. Even when we are fully ready and willing to sacrifice all that we have, even in these times of testing, we are to hold fast to the belief that somehow the promises of God will be fulfilled. We are to respond faithfully to God's call no matter what, no matter if we do not think we have the power to do so, no matter if we cannot understand why. In short, we are to be ready to respond even if we have to do without everything but our belief in God. To be so ready is one thing it means for God in Christ to be Lord of our histories.

Abraham was not always Abrahamic. He fell short on faithfulness; he was human. We will see this again and again as we rehearse the Biblical story. This story of Abraham's is found in Genesis Chapter 12. Since there was famine in the land, Abraham and his clan went to Egypt. Before they arrived he made a deal with Sarah, his wife. Sarah was beautiful to behold, and Abraham reckoned that the Egyptians would kill him and would let Sarah live. According to the deal, Sarah was to say that she was Abraham's sister, as he said, so "that it may go well with me because of you, and that my life may be spared on your account" (Genesis 12:13).

When she entered Egypt Sarah's beauty was appreciated. She was "taken into Pharaoh's house. And for her sake he dealt well with Abram; and he had sheep, oxen, he-asses, menservants, maidservants, she-asses, and camels" (Genesis 12:15-16).

In this story Abraham not only schemes to save his skin, but he also plots to secure his well-being and his possessions. These are not Abrahamic actions. These are not the actions of a man fully ready and willing to sacrifice everything just to be faithful to God's call.

Two promissory notes left above may now be redeemed. The question as to how we know that it is God who calls us, when we are called, may now be considered. The second note, to be discussed below, is the lamb that God said he would provide.

It is worth emphasizing that there has to be a concept of a call of God if we are to understand the Lordship of God. The call may be indirect, or it may be as it was with Abraham. It may be as it was later with Mary and Joseph, who were "warned in a dream." How the call comes is immaterial. What matters is that in some way there is a call. It is in calling us that God is exercising his Lordship for our lives. It is in calling us that God exercises a free initiative and that he guides us according to his purposes. Without some sort of call there would be nothing to show us what his purposes are, and therefore, nothing for us to respond to or to take as binding on our lives. Given a call, the question is how we know that it is God's call and that it is not some wish-fulfillment of our own.

It has already been noted what the explanation is that the general historian might give for Abraham's migration to the northwest. For the general historian there was a cause of the movement of the Amoritic people. Abraham, one of these people, understood the cause as a call from God. For the sacred historian, that is, for the man of faith, the cause of Abraham's movement was God's call to him. We do not accept the general historical explanation. Our question cannot be explained away.

One is tempted to answer the question by saying that if one asks whether or not it is God who is calling, then, it may be doubted that there has been a call from God. By analogy if we ask whether we really are in love, then we already have our negative answer. When God calls, we know that it is God who calls, just as when we truly are in love, we know that we are in love. When God calls we, like Abraham, know what we must do, for we cannot do otherwise. When we truly fall in love we know that we cannot do without the one we love.

This answer will not, however, silence the persistent question as to how we do know this. Abraham had much at stake if he was to follow God's call. And so may we, and if so we want some certainty that it is really God who is calling.

Our basic question concerns Lordship. In Abraham we have seen that in times of testing to let God exercise Lordship over us is to be fully ready and willing to do without everything. We are to rely totally on God's guidance and our belief that somehow the promises of God will be fulfilled. With Abraham we repeatedly stressed that he did not, indeed he could not, understand how these promises of God could be fulfilled if he did what God called him to do.

If we need to have certainty that it is God who is calling us, if we need some tests such that we can confirm that it is God's call, then God is not our Lord. He is not such because we seek some independent standard by which we determine that it is really God who is calling us. And we then, like Eve in the Garden, become little Gods knowing good and evil for ourselves.

This rebuttal of the persistent question perhaps is too harsh. Perhaps it is as I described in our times of testing, as it was with Abraham. But are there not some tests, which, in our everyday lives, we can use to have more confidence that it is God who is calling and not our own hidden wishes?

Some suggestions can be made. We can, like Abraham, respond faithfully and live with what we have done, letting the test of time confirm or disconfirm whether there really was a call from God. By analogy we can determine whether a love is true by the test of time. A relationship of two in love which lasts and flourishes over a period of time has, we can say, confirmed that it was and is a marriage of two people genuinely in love with one another.

By being faithful over what must have seemed a very long three days,

Abraham had confirmation that it was God who was calling. It was also God who confirmed his own call when he stopped Abraham who was ready with knife poised.

There are other suggestions. In an attitude of prayer the Biblical Christian can ask the Lord for a sign. Or he can take his calling into the fellowship of his Christian friends, being open for any judgment or criticism. Often in prayer in Christian fellowship with others it may be discerned whether a call is or is not genuinely a call from God. Christians can be sensitive to the spirit of God, or the lack of it, in the circle of fellowship.

These, then, are some practical common sense marks by which the Biblical Christian might test whether a call really is a call from God. These or other tests do not, however, give us certainty. To have this certainty is to take away the element of risk in the faithful following of God's call. We have seen in the story of Abraham that this risk was one of the important and necessary features of his response to God's calling to him.

The second promissory note may now be redeemed. This was the lamb mentioned by Abraham when he said to Isaac, "God will provide himself the lamb . . . , my son" (Genesis 22:8). By attending to the lamb we get an early glimpse of the unity of the whole sacred historical story in the Bible.

God promises to make a great nation of Abraham in a land that he will show him. That land, the holy land, was the land that God's people conquered and settled after going to Egypt, after the Exodus from Egypt under Moses, after forty years of wandering in the wilderness. The great nation was the nation occupying that land as it was unified under David. The savior, the Messiah, it was prophesied, was expected to come from the lineage of David to establish a kingdom by whom, as in God's promise to Abraham "all the families of the earth shall bless themselves" (Genesis 12:3).

God told Abraham that he would provide himself the lamb. His people were not ready for what God would provide. That would come in a later moment in the sacred historical story of God and his people. God did himself provide the lamb, in Jesus the Christ, the lamb of God who takes away the sins of the world.

B. Abrahamic Maturity

Out of the richness of the moment of the Abrahamic journey we can glean lessons concerning personal maturity. In his Noah moment the person searching for maturity emphasizes an independence and a self-sufficiency. He has an ability to stand on his own acting for what he judges best in spite of his separation, even condemnation and ridicule from others.

What of our Abrahamic moments in the drive for maturity? In these moments we live in a web of dependencies. If we are to be mature, however, we are to live on the threshold of readiness to step forth from this web to become independent. We become such at least to be free to do what we are called to do, that is, to sacrifice all that makes life comfortable and secure. We do this because as we did in our Noah moments we see a vision of a new society, a "great nation" by which "all the families of the earth shall bless themselves."

On this threshold we know our dependencies, say to our kinship system, yet we can become resigned to do without the same. In our Abrahamic moments of maturity we move from the dependencies to the resignation to the independence in a dynamic seasonal change in our spirits. All are Abrahamic.

So in the life of Abrahamic maturity we have to be sufficient unto ourselves to undergo these seasonal changes, these dynamic movements of the spirit. On the side of independence we must be practically wise to know what we must do to carry out our mission in life. As Abraham was we must be emotionally mature, to remain steady in our behavior in spite of terribly strong, even wrenching, feelings. In our Abrahamic moments this element of feelings is all the more pronounced because of the blockage of common sense or reason. We are in a bind in our Abrahamic moments in that we cannot understand how we can be faithful to what we are called to do if, in fact, we do it. We do have the capacity for making practically wise judgments about what our mission is, but our reason is limited. The Abrahamically mature person can not fully understand what he is doing.

Also on the side of independence is the Abrahamic social maturity. In this we act according to acceptable social standards of behavior given our dependence. However, when we recognize our call to mission we know that we are called by a higher power to depart from the ordinary. Abraham departed from the ordinary by taking his journey in faith, leaving "his earthly understandings behind him." What power moves a person searching for maturity on such a journey? In the Biblical or sacred historical Abrahamic moment the movement is a response to a call of God. Yet as a moment of testing it is not God who moves Abraham. He has to move himself, and in this sense also he is independent. For the man in search of maturity there is also this independent impetus. He goes on the journey not because of the dictates of his own practically wise judgments, not because of his feelings that he wants to go, not because it is socially acceptable to go. He goes, not knowing why. He goes out of an impetus to fulfill a vision; yet he does not know how this can be fulfilled. The future pulls him, and he decides to go with it. He does undertake the journey. There is independence in this act.

In the Abrahamic maturity there is nothing of the self-sufficiency we found in the Noah moment of maturity. In the Abrahamic times of testing there needs to be an independence as we have seen. Yet for a person tested, who is moving towards a future he knows not what and who must be willing to sacrifice so much, there is no complete self-sufficiency. Unlike Noah the Abrahamically mature man is not sufficient in himself. He does not stand alone to complete the task he was called to perform. He is pulled towards a future, towards a promise of a "great nation," but he does not fully understand how what he is doing will help him to gain the objective of his difficult journey.

We have seen the senses in which the Abrahamically mature person is independent, but not self-sufficient. The dependencies in the Abrahamic quest for maturity are also noteworthy. In that he showed practical wisdom in recognizing the call he was independent. That he lacked understanding in following this call shows a dependency to that which called him to the future which pulls him. Although he is emotionally steady in his journey the Abrahamic person has surrendered himself to that which impels him towards his destination. Although he is socially mature in that he does what is socially acceptable except when he had good reason to do otherwise, this social maturity, too, was lost. The person mature after Abraham does that which is not socially acceptable, and his "good reason" for doing what he is doing is a reason he himself cannot understand. He sets aside his practical wisdom, his good reasons, his sense of right. Such are not the actions of a socially mature person.

In Abrahamic maturity there is a sense not only of dependence but of absolute dependence, or, as I have called it, self-insufficiency. The Abrahamically mature person has lost or suspended his practical wisdom, has set aside his personal feelings and emotions in a kind of "infinite resignation," and he has stepped out of socially acceptable and normal patterns of behavior. In these three senses he has become self-insufficient. He is also absolutely dependent on the pull from the future, on the vision of the "great nation" which will, he believes, be made of him. This is not something he can explain to his son who is to be sacrificed or to his wife who bore that son. This is not something social. It is the belief of the Abrahamically mature person who has acted independently and who also in his act has chosen to be absolutely dependent.

Abraham is mature simply because he can stand out from his web of dependencies and be independent when in his practical wisdom the occasion requires it. He is mature also just because he can give himself away and be dependent, even self-insufficient. The language of maturity in the Abrahamic moment apart from a Biblical Christian context concerns the dynamic between independence on the one hand and dependence, even self-insufficiency on the other hand. The Abrahamic person is mature just and only because he can choose to move to and from the poles of this dynamic movement of the spirit.

4

The Exodus Moment

A. Moses and the Exodus

In the sacred historical moment of Moses and the Exodus there is the first clear indication that God acts in relation to a people, the people who will in the covenant at Sinai become his people. This moment marks the beginning of the sacred historical relation God has with his people as a nation. Hosea seems to suggest this in writing, "When Israel was a child, I loved him, and out of Egypt I called my son" (Hosea 11:1). This view also is contained in what probably is an ancient Biblical source, which we may call the Deuteronomic confession of faith.

> And you shall make response before the Lord your God, "A wandering Aramean was my father; and he went down to Egypt and sojourned there, few in number; and there he became a nation, great, mighty, and populous. And the Egyptians treated us harshly, and afflicted us, and laid upon us hard bondage. Then we cried to the Lord the God of our fathers, and the Lord heard our voice, and saw our affliction, our toil, and our oppression; and the Lord brought us out of Egypt with a mighty hand and an outstretched arm, with great terror, with signs and wonders; and he brought us into this place and gave us this land, a land flowing with milk and honey. And behold, now I bring the first of the fruit of the ground, which thou, O Lord, has given me."
>
> (Deuteronomy 26:5-10a)

The people of God are made one as God frees them as one from bondage. They were slaves in the Egyptian social system. He brought them out of Egypt with a mighty hand. In the sacred historical story of God and his people, the exodus means the great saving act of God in freeing the people from bondage, in making a people in this act, and of leading them towards the Promised Land.

The story of Moses and the exodus is told in the book of Exodus, beginning in Chapter 2, with the birth of Moses. It is not necessary to rehearse all the details of the story of Moses's birth as a Hebrew, of his rearing in the court of Pharaoh, of the incident in which he killed an Egyptian taskmaster who was beating a Hebrew, and of his flight from Pharaoh's Egypt to Midian, the land of Jethro, priest of Midian.

There is, however, one incident recounted in Exodus, Chapter 3, where Moses meets God on Horeb, the mountain. On this we will dwell, for from it we learn much about what it is for God to be Lord. It is not God himself who appears to Moses on the mountain, but an angel of the Lord (Exodus 3:2). The angel appears "in a flame of fire out of the midst of a bush" (Exodus 3:2).

In this incident Moses is in the presence of God, who himself remains absent.

25

Here is a primary ingredient of one of the traditional attributes or characteristics of God, that is, his Holiness. God is present, yet he remains hidden as in a great mystery. And in the presence of the Holy One there are signs and wonders. Moses looked, and "lo, the bush was burning, yet it was not consumed" (Exodus 3:2).

God called to Moses: "Do not come near" (Exodus 3:5). The Holy One is not to be approached. "Put off your shoes from your feet, for the place on which you are standing is holy ground" (Exodus 3:5). "And Moses hid his face, for he was afraid to look at God" (Exodus 3:6). Not only is God the Holy One hidden as in a great mystery, not only are there signs and wonders in his presence, but also there is fear. In the presence of the Holy One one is overwhelmed and over-powered. One is afraid. One has a sense of awe.

God, the Holy One, identifies himself. "I am the God of your father, the God of Abraham, the God of Isaac, and the God of Jacob" (Exodus 3:6). God tells Moses what he has seen of the affliction and suffering of the people in Egypt, and of how he is going to bring them out of Egypt into a "good and broad land, a land flowing with milk and honey" (Exodus 3:8), and of how Moses is going to lead them.

Moses wants to know the name of God. He wants to know more of who this God is. "God said to Moses, 'I am who I am' " (Exodus 3:14). This name could be translated otherwise to read 'I will be what I will be' or yet again 'I cause to be what I cause to be.'

What kind of name is this? No name at all, really. God the Holy One is iden-tifying himself as the one who is, who will be what he will be, who will cause to happen what he causes to happen. It is not possible for us to know who he is, or what he will be or what he will cause to happen unless he reveals it to us. What he does reveal to Moses in this hour is that he is to go out into the world doing the work of his God, who is his Lord.

From the incident of Moses on the mountain we learn much of what it is for God in Christ to be Lord of our histories. There will be times in our sacred historical relationships to him in which we will meet him as Moses met him on the mountain. He will be present, yet absent, hidden in the mystery. There will be signs and wonders. We will be afraid, overpowered, overwhelmed and full of awe. We will be full of our own powerlessness. We will have the feeling of being a creature before the Other who is our creator, as did the man and the woman in the Garden before the fall. We will have the feeling of being absolutely dependent or self-insufficient. What we will know of God is just that he is, that he will be, and that he will cause to be what he will cause to be. The course of our history, and ultimately of general history itself, is in his hands. We will know that our one and only task is to be faithful to his word for us. Thus he will be our Lord.

Having been convinced that God was with him, by the sign of the rod becom-ing a serpent (Exodus 4:2-9), and by the fact that Aaron would be with him and would speak for him to the people (Exodus 4:16), Moses went back to Egypt to confront Pharaoh.

In Exodus Chapter 5 they went to Pharaoh asking only that they could take the people of God and go "a three day's journey into the wilderness, and sacrifice to the Lord our God" (Exodus 5:3). This reflects one account of the exodus, that the objective was a less modest one than the Promised Land itself. Pharaoh said "no", and increased their work load in the brick factory (Exodus 5:7).

God, who declared himself to be the same God who appeared to Abraham,

Isaac and Jacob, but who did not make his name known to them (Exodus 6:2-3), affirmed that he would bring the people out of Egypt, delivering them from their bondage (Exodus 6:6).

Moses and Aaron went to Pharaoh again. God would repeatedly harden Pharaoh's heart (Exodus 7:3), yet he would bring the people out of Egypt (Exodus 7:5). There followed the contests between Moses and Pharaoh, contests between the signs given by God and the willingness of Pharaoh to let the people go. First there were the rods (Exodus 7:8-12). But still Pharaoh's heart was hardened. Then came the ten plagues: the blood (Exodus 7:17 ff), the frogs (Exodus 8:2 ff), the gnats (Exodus 8:16 ff), the flies (Exodus 8:21 ff), the plague on the cattle (Exodus 9:3 ff), the boils (Exodus 9:9), the hail (Exodus 9:18 ff), the locusts (Exodus 10:4), and the darkness (Exodus 10:21 ff).

Finally came the worst plague of all, the death of the first born of Egypt, "from the first-born of Pharaoh who sits upon his throne, even to the first born of the maidservant who is behind the mill and all the first born of the cattle" (Exodus 11:5). The Lord "smote all the first-born in the land of Egypt" (Exodus (12:29 ff). Pharaoh summoned Moses and said, "Be gone" (Exodus 12:32). "And on that very day the Lord brought the people of Israel out of the land of Egypt" (Exodus 12:51).

Immediately, the people celebrated with the feast of unleavened bread (Exodus 13:1-10). They went out of the land of Egypt. "And the Lord went before them by day in a pillar of cloud to lead them along the way, and by night in a pillar of fire to give them light" (Exodus 13:21). Again God hardened the heart of Pharaoh (Exodus 14:8), and Pharaoh pursued the people. Israel moved between the waters of the sea (Exodus 14:21-25), and when the Egyptians pursued, the water came back upon them. And "the Lord routed the Egyptians in the midst of the sea" (Exodus 14:27).

"Thus the Lord saved Israel that day from the hand of the Egyptians (Exodus 14:30). And Moses and the people celebrated in song (Exodus 15:1-18). And Miriam sang her song of triumph (Exodus 15:21). "Then Moses led Israel onward from the Red Sea . . ." (Exodus 15:22).

In this sacred historical moment we can see clearly something of what it is for God in Christ to be Lord of our histories. God delivered the people from bondage in Egypt. So in our Christian lives do we have the experience of being freed from bondage, freed from our sins which bind us, freed from our old ways which restrict us. The Exodus moment in our Christian faith is the liberating moment of being a new creation in the eyes of God, the moment when the past is finished and gone, and everything is fresh and new. So as individuals we know the liberating effects of God's activity in our individual sacred histories. We know it also in God's Lordship over the Church.

B. The Exodus, Passover and Lord's Supper

The people of God celebrated the Passover prior to their Exodus from Egypt. Today the Jew remembers and relives the events of the Exodus in the Passover. Today Christians remember and relive the sacrifice of Jesus Christ in the celebration of the Lord's Supper in the Church. The indispensable link between these two events is that for Jews and Christians each is the crucial historical experience of a people becoming a community.

There is another link. The Jew sees himself participating anew in the experience of the Exodus from Egypt. "In every generation," so goes part of the Passover ritual, "it is the duty of a man to imagine that he himself has come forth from Egypt."

So the other link is a matter of time. In the present event one remembers and relives the past and hopes for the future. Like the Jew, the Christian, in celebrating the Lord's Supper, participates in a present event in which he remembers the past and anticipates the future. Christians hope for the kingdom of heaven. Jews hope for freedom in the Promised Land.

All this is built into the Passover ritual in the part of the service most sacred to the Jew, namely the Seder prayer. As one eats the different foods the children ask questions such as the following: "Why is this night different from all the other nights? . . . On all other nights, we eat all kinds of herbs; on this night, we especially eat bitter herbs."[1] The answers are explained by the wisest old Jew as the young and old eat a meal in remembrance of the bitter days in the desert and remind themselves of the persecution of the Jewish people throughout history. But in the prayer they also remember and relive the experience of being brought as a people out of Egypt. They relive their experience of freedom.

So also it is with communion in the Christian Church. We believe that in the Lord's Supper we commune together as a body of Christians with the real presence of Christ, who frees us as a people from bondage. There is a parallel, therefore, between the exodus moment in our sacred histories as the Church and as individual Christians. The exodus experience of being freed from all that binds us can be interpreted as applying to us as individuals or to the Church as a body.

C. The Maturity of Freedom

In the quest for maturity bondage is a problem. In the sacred historical story the people of God were held bondage in Egypt. They were unfree. They were dependent on the Egyptians, their taskmasters. Insofar as they were slaves in the Egyptian social system they were self-insufficient, unable to take any sort of independent positions for themselves. In their situation there was no true community, for their social status and relation was entirely determined by outside forces. There could be no moments for them of Noah-like independence and self-sufficiency. There could be no Abrahamic moments of independence and also the dynamic shift in the spirit to a dependence, even a self-insufficiency. Such is the problem of bondage in the quest for maturity.

In the exodus season of the spirit there is a freedom from this problematic bondage. There are the conditions created for independent exercises of man's powers. The conditions are created for a recovery of true community, for the making of a people as one, even for the making of a "great nation" as envisioned by a person in his Abrahamic moment of maturity. In the life of the person searching for maturity there will come times when he is freed from bondage. To become mature is to know such liberating experiences.

The bondage may be cognitive or intellectual. Often people searching for maturity are bound in the context of a set of beliefs or dispositions of mind which are entirely received and as such unexamined. These beliefs will be unquestioned; they may even be tacit or unrecognized. Indeed as was the case with the people of God in bondage in Egypt a person might not be in a position to question them. Their binding force or the manner in which they were received might preclude such questioning and reflection. In such intellectual bondage a person is immature in that he cannot or does not exercise independent practical judgments.

Again immature persons may be seen as those bound by strong, even uncontrollable, feelings. Insofar as a person may be in intellectual bondage he is unable to exercise his practical reason as a steadying or controlling or regulating force on the feelings. Thus his bondage may be deep. He may just not be able to recognize a feeling as in a nameless anxiety. Or again he may not be able to face a feeling and deal or cope with it, as, for example, in the fear of flying.

Thirdly, there may be a bondage which is social, a bondage to certain forms of relationships, behavioral habits or social mores. There is a crystal clear reflection of such bondage in the enslavement of the people of God in Egypt. Such bondage may be reflected in the saying of a dying social institution—"We've never done it that way before." This could be aptly described as "the seven last words" of such a social unit. If morals is defined as the application of culturally acceptable forms of behavior to one's life, then the bound person might well be understood to be the fully moral man. Such a person would, by definition, be unable to freely and rationally think for himself what is ethically right, apart from the moral standards of his culture.

An immature person enslaved cognitively or emotionally or socially lives in a radical self-insufficiency. There is an immaturity involved in the life of such a person, for in such a bound state there cannot be any real independence, no free exercise of one's reason or feelings. Thus there can be no dynamic movement between dependence and independence of which the mature life is made. There is no freedom of mind, heart or social behavior.

In the exodus season of the spirit in the person searching for maturity he will be led out of a time of self-insufficiency into a time of independence in which he may display the three kinds of maturity, intellectual, emotional and social. The exodus moment in the mature life is the moment when such conditions are manifest.

In the sacred historical story the moment of the exodus was the moment not only when God freed his people, but also the moment in which he made his people one people. So likewise in the life in search of maturity can this moment of liberation allow the mature man to enter freely into the web of dependencies in his culture—his family, friends and associates. Before, the natural man was bound and enslaved in a personal bondage. Now, after the exodus season of the spirit, he has been made independent and free to become dependent upon his people.

It is just this dynamic of independence and dependence which is experienced in the Seder Prayer in the Jewish passover service and the Lord's Supper in the Christian Church. In these riturals one relives the freedom in the exodus season of the spirit; one also is bound to the people in the Synagogue or Church.

The maturity of freedom is thus a two-fold phenomenon. On the one hand there is the liberation of an individual person from a state in which his power to act rationally, emotionally and socially acceptably or unacceptably is nil. This liberation allows again for personal independence and, therefore, for the person's ability to move dynamically, like an Abrahamic man, from independence to dependence, even in their radical forms. On the other hand there is the formation of a people in the act of liberation. There are the conditions for the creation of social maturity in a social system composed of rules and restrictions freely chosen. As in the Jewish and Christian religious services of Passover and Communion the very experience of liberation is social or corporate. In this exodus liberating season of the spirit in the quest for maturity, one realizes that one does not become mature all by oneself.

This exodus experience of liberation will not come quickly or easily. Strange and even incomprehensible things will have to happen to shake us loose from binding dispositions of mind or patterns of behavior. There will be social restrictions which make it very difficult to realize a system of close social bonds. Everyone will be burdened down with his own work which he has to do.

The "great nation" envisioned in our Abrahamic moments in the quest for maturity will only become a reality if we are liberated from our bondage. In our radical self-insufficiency in the exodus moment this liberation will not happen because of our choice. It will be, as it was in our Abrahamic moment, that we will be pulled into the future as if by a greater power than ourselves. By that power, which is hidden from us as if in a cloud of smoke on a mountain top, we will be freed. This exodus liberation of the spirit will be accompanied by "signs and wonders" which we do not understand but which cause us to rejoice greatly. There will be more joy in this moment of maturity than we have so far known.

5

The Wilderness and Law Moments

A. The First Moment in the Wilderness

The people of God were freed from bondage. Freed for what? They were freed from all those things they had been used to, even if they had been treated like slaves. In the Egyptian system they at least knew their place.

But what were they freed for? The first moment in the wilderness is the moment between the exodus and the giving of the law. In this moment the people did not yet know what they were freed for. They, like Abraham, did not know where they were going or what they were headed for.

In their absolute freedom under the providence of God they were in the wilderness, which may be seen as a wilderness of the spirit. There was nothing which bound them, nothing which gave them an identity as a people. They had no clarity of purpose as a people. Thus was their wilderness.

We will see this wilderness of the spirit, this nothingness, this lack of identification, again and again in the rehearsal. It was before the creation of the world, in which God established a relationship with us as his creatures. It was with the people in the wilderness, it was with the people in the fall of Jerusalem. It was with the disciples after the crucifixion of Jesus and before the resurrection.

From all these Biblical instances of being in the wilderness of the spirit, we learn something about Lordship. We may be in a wilderness. We may know what we have been freed from but not what we have been freed for. We may, like Abraham, have nothing to go by but the promises of God. There will be these times of trial of our faith. The lesson, however, is that God is with us, God is still guiding us towards the fulfillment of his purposes even as we are in the wilderness of the spirit.

The people had been freed from bondage in Egypt, a system in which their place was known. Now they had been freed from that place. They did not know who they were. They sometimes did not know where their next meal was coming from. At one point in the wilderness before the law had been given, some said that it was better for them to be slaves in Egypt than to starve in the wilderness (Exodus 14:11,12).

Also they did not know exactly where they were going, except that it was a Promised Land. Moses told them that God was leading them. And God was with them preparing them to live in a state of absolute dependence on him. In the wilderness of their lives, they had nothing but the promises of God to sustain them. No matter how hard it was for them to understand their plight, God was with them still.

B. The Moment When the Law was Given

In the sacred historical story of the people of God the giving of the law means this: that the people are defined by, and regulated by, the law of God given by God to the people.

In Exodus a covenant is made between God and Moses for the people. God calls Moses and says, "Thus you shall say to the house of Jacob, and tell the people of Israel: You have seen what I did to the Egyptians, and how I bore you on eagles' wings and brought you to myself. Now therefore, if you will obey my voice and keep my covenant, you shall be my own possession among all peoples; for all the earth is mine, and you shall be to me a kingdom of priests and a holy nation. These are the words which you shall speak to the children of Israel" (Exodus 19:3-6).

So Moses told God's message to the elders of the people. And God came to them in a thick cloud, again suggesting his holiness. And the covenant was made (Exodus 19:9-20). The people were consecrated, their garments were washed (Exodus 19:14), and they were told to be ready, which readiness, interestingly, includes the injunction not to "go near a woman" (Exodus 19:15).

Then the Bible says, "On the morning of the third day" (Exodus 19:16) God came to the people, yet again suggesting his holiness, in "thunders and lightnings, and a thick cloud upon the mountain, and a very loud trumpet blast, so that all the people who were in the camp trembled" (Exodus 19:16).

The people came out of the camp to meet God, taking their stand at the foot of the mountain. "And Mount Sinai was wrapped in smoke, because the Lord descended upon it in fire" (Exodus 19:18). The Lord came to the top of the mountain, calling Moses to come up, telling him to warn the people "lest they break through to the Lord to gaze and many of them perish" (Exodus 19:21). Moses did what he was told. Then God spoke his words to Moses and Aaron, giving them his law, first in the form of the Ten Commandments (Exodus 20:2-17).

In this moment in the sacred historical story God gives his law to his people, and we are defined by it, regulated by it, and identified by it. We are the people of the law, and what it is for us to be faithful is now to follow God's law. In so doing we are keeping the covenant he has made with us. He is our Lord, and we are his people. We have regained an identification, a purpose which we had lost in the first moment in the wilderness. Our lives now have meaning and direction, and we know what it is to be faithful, whether that be by following the spirit or the letter of the law or both.

Let it not be thought that by entering into a covenant, an agreement with God, we are in any way limiting his Lordship over us. We are to be his people only if we follow his law. And he gives his law unconditionally. There are, for example, laws about buying Hebrew slaves (Exodus 21:2-6), which are phrased in if-then language. There are also laws in the form of staccato commands, e.g. "Whoever curses his father or his mother shall be put to death" (Exodus 21:17). The former type of law may be called conditional: If x happens then y will be the legal consequence. For the most part, the law of the Lord is unconditional or absolute, befitting his Lordship. The Ten Commandments are categorical commands, e.g. "You shall not steal." They express the unconditional commands of the covenant God has made with his people.

So we are to be his people, and we acknowledge him as Lord only if we keep his unconditional laws made by him in the form of categorical commands. For

God in Christ to be Lord we must be prepared, like Noah, Abraham and Moses to follow God's commandments without even a thought of the consequences.

Our covenant with God is not an agreement between equals. The covenant is given by God unconditionally, and he is our Lord only if we follow it the same way. Only then is God in Christ our Lord. That our covenant does not limit the Lordship of God can be seen in yet another way: God enters into his covenant with us, but he, himself, is not bound by it.

C. The Second Moment in the Wilderness

We do not follow the law of the Lord in this way. We are like the woman in the Garden, Noah and Abraham. We all fall short in faithfulness. After having been made a people by God's act of freeing us from bondage in the exodus and after his act of giving us his law, we still look out for ourselves. We still have to develop a sense of being a people of God who live under the Lordship of God in Christ.

After the exodus, after the receiving of the law, there was a time of wandering in the wilderness prior to the entrance into the Promised Land. This period in the sacred history is a period in which the people continued to develop as one people under God. During this time the Lord God showed himself in unique ways. He supplied daily sustenance in the form of manna and quail (See Exodus 16:1-36). God was with the people in the wilderness giving them in those days their daily bread. He supplied them with water from the rock at Horeb (Exodus 17:6). His guidance was also shown in the fierce struggle of the people for survival against the military strength of others, such as the Amalekites (Exodus 17:8-10).

We see here, as we have seen before and as we will see again, that we are to be dependent on God in Christ and on him alone. From this second moment in the wilderness we learn that God even supplies our daily bread. Our job is not to be concerned with what we shall eat, or what we shall drink, or what we shall put on. If God in Christ is Lord of our sacred histories we are not, like the woman in the garden, to want to know for ourselves what is good for our food. Our one and only job is to seek first the kingdom of God.

The oneness of the people of God is not to be achieved in the wilderness. This is to be a state of preparation. The process of unification of the people, which began in the exodus, which continued in the wilderness, will not soon be achieved. It will not come until the savior of the world comes in David's image to establish God's kingdom, which is not finally to be realized until the end of time.

The time in the wilderness, the second moment in the wilderness, is clearly different from the first wilderness moment. In the first instance we are in a wilderness of the spirit, a condition in which we know the bondage we have been freed from but not the service we have been freed for. The first spiritual wilderness is a meaningless, purposeless, absolute freedom.

After we are given the law of God, the second wilderness moment has a different character. We no longer live in an absolutely free state. We have been given a new bondage, a new law which binds us, a new identification and purpose which guides us. We have been given God's law.

We are in a wilderness, however, for we fall short of faithfully following that law and we are conscious of our shortcomings. As Paul is later to say, what does knowledge of the law bring but consciousness of our own sin? (Romans 7:7). The second moment in the wilderness is a moment of judgment in which we live under the judgment of God and of our own awareness of our lack of faith.

In the sacred historical Biblical story this element of judgment is clearly depicted in the book of Numbers. The people complain "in the hearing of the Lord" about their misfortunes (Numbers 11:1). In Egypt "we had meat to eat! . . . the leeks, the onions . . . ; but now there is nothing at all but this to look at" (Numbers 11:4-6). We take thought and are desirous, not of the kingdom of God and his righteousness, but of what we have to eat.

We grumble as did the people in the wilderness. Indeed the second wilderness of the spirit is a time of grumbling. There is the judgment of God for our unfaithfulness during this time, for when the Lord hears our grumblings his "anger" is "kindled" (Numbers 11:1). Yet the Lord will give us meat, and we shall eat (Numbers 11:18). Even in his judgment the Lord has mercy on us, and he loves us. He brings what we want in the wind. "And there went forth a wind from the Lord, and it brought quails from the sea" (Numbers 11:31).

We murmur against the prophets of God: "Would that we had died in the land of Egypt" (Numbers 14:2). Would that we had lived and died in bondage. Would that we had never known the liberating and mighty deed of the exodus, in which God, the Lord, frees us and binds us for his service. We long for the old ways, which, however burdensome, were at least secure. We all love our security, and with our inadequate faith we are afraid to take Abrahamic risks, afraid to and unprepared to follow God's call into an uncertain future, just to be faithful to him.

And we do not escape the judgment of God. "Then the Lord said, 'I have pardoned . . . ; but truly, as I live, and as all the earth shall be filled with the glory of the Lord, none of the men who have seen my glory and my signs which I wrought in Egypt and in the wilderness, and yet have put me to the proof these ten times and have not hearkened to my voice, shall see the land which I swore to give to their fathers; and none of those who despised me shall see it" (Numbers 14:20-23).

About Moses and Aaron God wonders, "How long shall this wicked congregation murmur against me?" (Numbers 14:27). God levels his judgment: "But as for you, your dead bodies shall fall in this wilderness. And your children shall be shepherds in the wilderness forty years, and shall suffer for your faithlessness" (Numbers 14:32-33).

Moses and Aaron themselves did not escape the judgment of God. Like the woman in the garden, like Noah and Abraham, they fell short in faithfulness. They glorified themselves, and they did not sanctify the Lord God in the eyes of the people (See Numbers 20:1-13). They chose to elevate themselves to the rank of God and, thereby, failed to acknowledge the Lordship of God in Christ. Because of their sin at the waters of Meribah neither Moses nor Aaron was to enter the Promised Land. Moses did see it from the mountains of Transjordan before he died (See Deuteronomy 34). What a bittersweet experience that must have been for him, to see, like all of us at one time or another, the promises of God fulfilled before our eyes, and yet at the same time to know his judgment on us for our unfaithfulness.

D. The Problem of Freedom

From the Exodus, the first moment in the wilderness and the giving of the law, from these three moments in the sacred historical story, there is raised the problem of freedom. It might be put as follows: absolute freedom is meaningless, since freedom necessarily includes bondage to something. If this is the case, then what sort of freedom, if any at all, does man have?

In the discussion of the problem of evil in Section 10, I will argue that evil originates in the exercise of man's free capacity to choose not to do what God has called him to do and be. That such free choice is available was supported by reference to the choice of the woman in the garden, which is, of course, man's own choice to elevate himself to the rank of Lord over his own life.

In the discussion of the problem of spiritual and moral autonomy it will be shown that self-consciousness must be sacrificed if God is to be Lord. From the moments in the garden before the fall it has been learned that in the state in which God in Christ is Lord men are bound to do what he calls them to do and be, but they are free to do and be otherwise.

This is, in a sense, a negative freedom, the freedom not to be faithful. This freedom will be consistent with the solution to the problem of "the others." The negative freedom also was evident in the wilderness, between the moments in bondage in Egypt and the moment in which man was rebound to the law. Is the Biblical Christian free in any positive sense?

E. The Maturity of Bondage

In the quest for maturity, freedom is a problem. The mature person knows moments of liberation from binding habits or dispositions in his exodus season of the spirit. After liberation, then what? The mature man, like the Biblical Christian, may know full well what he has been freed from but not what he has been freed for. Thus he too is in a kind of wilderness of the spirit.

This wilderness is a kind of psychological gap in the passage from bondage to freedom and to bondage again. In this point in the quest for maturity it is the freedom which is the problem. Being freed from our intellectual, emotional and social binds in the exodus moment of the spirit raises a question. As with the people freed in the sacred historical story, the person questing for maturity may ask these questions: where am I now; what am I now; where am I going now?

In this wilderness moment of the spirit in the life of one seeking maturity, there is lacking that essential dynamic between dependence and independence, even between self-insufficiency and self-sufficiency. Before the liberating exodus moment, as we have seen, there was in the bondage a radical dependence. In the first wilderness moment after such liberation there is no independence or self-sufficiency. There is no independent making of practically wise judgments about what is best for one's life. There is no new set of feelings or emotionally definable states of mind. The one feeling might be that of being lost. There is no new pattern of behavior independently arrived at. There is no practical judgment as to what is socially acceptable and what is not. There is the problem of freedom, the problem of any meaning or form of this lack of bondage. There is the question as to whether this freedom has any meaning at all. It appears to be absolute, such as in a state of unlimited license. In it one's life appears to have no purpose, for there is no sense of direction. In a sense, then, the problem of freedom is this: in this state of absolute freedom from any restrictions is there any meaning or purpose at all?

The problem of freedom in the first moment in the wilderness is solved by a re-identification, a re-orientation of the person and of the society of which he is a part. Prior to the exodus liberation the people were bound, intellectually, emotionally and socially. Now in the moment of the law they are re-bound. In the sacred historical story this means that God had given them the law, and they became the people of the law. In the life of developing maturity this means that a person acquires new and newly binding intellectual and emotional dispositions of mind and a new set of socially acceptable rules by which to live. Such solve the problem. Suddenly there are restrictions and rules. Consequently there is a sense of meaning and purpose—to live in accordance with these rules and restrictions. Ironically there is the need of such new binds before there can be the independent making of practically wise judgments which give a new stability to one's emotional and social life.

In the sacred historical story these new bounds are given by God as a set of categorical commands, which are to be followed unconditionally. Thus there is a radical bondage here, a self-insufficiency to devise rules of one's own. In the developing life of maturity at this moment of the giving of the law there must be an act of independence, of independently devising new rules, new habits, new forms of behavior. Such redefinition of life must be done for oneself and one's people out of a wilderness moment of the spirit. As in the Noah mature moment it is a kind of new beginning.

The second wilderness moment in the spirit of one searching for maturity is a moment of freedom. Yet it is not absolute and meaningless as was the first moment. We now know both what binds us and what we can be free from. We now know that in our freedom we fall short of faithfully following the new set of intellectual judgments, emotional disposition and social forms of behavior that we ourselves have set up.

It is not a happy or easy moment, certainly not as it was in our exodus experience. We grumble even against ourselves. We still are divided against each other in our newly constructed social environment. We wander about in life spinning our wheels, knowing what we ought to be and do but living under our own judgment that we have failed to live up to these standards of the best for us.

The passage from bondage to freedom to bondage and back to freedom is complex indeed. The first bondage, in our Egypt moment of the spirit, is radical. In this we are self-insufficient, having no freedom for the mature exercise of, for example, our own practical judgments as to what is best. We move from this bound state to an absolute, meaningless purposeless freedom in which we have lost any sense of direction and any self-identification. This freedom is absolute and meaningless, for in it there is no possibility of a spiritual dynamic between dependence and independence.

From this negatively free state we move to a new identification under the guidance of new rules, dispositions and new forms of behavior. We have devised these out of our independence and we become willingly dependent upon them. Thus we are rebound. Yet we fall short in faithfulness to them. In our independent judgment we know our own failures. We are, in this moment in the wilderness, discontent with ourselves.

6

The Moments in the Land Flowing with Milk and Honey

A. The Moments of the Conquest, Settlement and the Judges

In the Bible there are two accounts of the conquest and settlement in the land that God had shown his people. The first is given in the book of Joshua, Chapters 1 through 12. The conquest is pictured as swift and destructive, with successful attacks on the center, south and north. The second account, given in the opening chapters of the book of Judges, is much different. Here there is no single leader. The various tribes among the people operate individually, and the conquest is not quickly successful. It is more like an infiltration.

As a moment in the sacred history, the conquest and the settlement is that time in which the people came to that land that God said he would show to Abraham. The conditions for the fulfillment of God's promises required that the people would dwell in the land to which he would lead them. In this homecoming there is a rekindling of the hope that the promises of God will be fulfilled. There is celebration and thanksgiving that the people have settled in the land given them by God, this land, which, in the words of the Deuteronomic Confession, was a land "flowing with milk and honey" (Deuteronomy 26:9). The people are so thankful that they bring "the first of the fruit of the ground" which the Lord God had given to them (Deuteronomy 26:10).

The people had looked forward to and longed for this land, and they were filled with hope as they anticipated God's Holy Land. "For the Lord your God is bringing you into a good land, a land of brooks, of water, . . . flowing forth in valleys and hills, . . . a land in which you will eat bread without scarcity, in which you will lack nothing, a land whose stones are iron and out of whose hills you can dig copper" (Deuteronomy 8:7,9). And God had told them, "You shall eat and be full, and you shall bless the Lord your God for the good land he has given you" (Deuteronomy 8:10).

The first account of the conquest symbolizes the faith we have in the power of God to fulfill his promises. We know, as did the people of old, what it is to be bound to hard bondage in a system that enslaves us. We have known the mighty liberating effects of having been freed from this bondage by God's power, and in our exodus moment of the spirit, there are again the mighty acts of God symbolized in signs and wonders all about us. We know also the moment in the wilderness when we have been freed from bondage. We have been given God's law, which identifies us as a people who do not forget the Lord our God by failing to keep "his commandments and his ordinances and his statutes" which he has given us (Deuteronomy 8:11). Yet we also have known the awful judgment of God for our unfaithfulness, and we have suffered for our lack of faith by meandering through life with no clear sense of purpose. But now the promises of God are fulfilled before our eyes. For all that God has done we give thanks, we rejoice, we sing his praises, we celebrate in a joy of fulfillment, yet in a joy filled with anticipation and hope. For in this season of the spirit in the conquest and settlement we find our home, and we can live in that place where God intended that we live. It is the promised land of our lives, that place in which we can serve, where we can live under the Lordship of God in Christ.

It is a time when we settle. It is a season when, on occasion, we need to rehearse our histories, to know from whence we came. It is a time for occasional renewal. It is a time when others join us, particularly those in the land to which God has brought us. These occur in what we might call a covenant renewal ceremony (See Joshua 24).

All through this period of the judges the Biblical story is dominated by what we might call the Deuteronomic success formula. This is clearly stated in Judges 2:6—3:6, and it runs as follows: Joshua, the leader, dismissed the people from a gathering, and each went "to his inheritance to take possession of the land" (Judges 2:6). Joshua died, and after that there arose another generation who did not know the work the Lord had done.

The people "did what was evil in the sight of the Lord. . . . So the anger of the Lord was kindled against Israel, and he gave them over to plunderers, who plundered them. . . . Then the Lord raised up judges, who saved them out of the power of those who plundered them. . . . And he saved them from the hand of their enemies all the days of the judge. . . . But whenever the judge died, they turned back and behaved worse than their fathers. . . . So the anger of the Lord was kindled against" the people (Judges 2:11-20). Again the people did what was evil in the sight of the Lord. And so the cycle continues through all the stories in the book of Judges.

During the sacred historical story from the exodus out of Egypt, the giving of the law, the time in the wilderness, the conquest and settlement, during all this time the people of God had not as yet become one people. A quite revealing characterization of the times and of confirmation of the divisions of the people, of the judges, is found in the last sentence of the book of Judges: "In those days there was no king in Israel; every man did what was right in his own eyes" (Judges 21:25).

The Deuteronomic success formula may be seen as just another way of saying that we are to be dependent on God and on him alone. "The imagination of man is evil from his youth." The power of man to save himself, apart from the Lordship of God in Christ, is nil.

B. A King in Israel:The Moments from Samuel to Saul to David

Samuel could be called the last of the judges, except that he was not primarily a military champion as were the others. Mainly he was the prophet who spoke the word of the Lord to the people.

The account of Samuel's birth is given in I Samuel Chapter 1. In Chapter 2 it is recounted how a man of God tells Eli, the faithful priest, that he will raise up one "who shall do according to what is in my heart and in my mind; and I will build him a sure house, and he shall go in and out before my anointed forever" (I Samuel 2:35). This is Samuel, who "was ministering to the Lord under Eli" in the days when "the word of the Lord was rare" (I Samuel 3:1).

Samuel was called by God in I Samuel Chapter 3, and he "grew, and the Lord was with him and let none of his words fall to the ground. And all Israel from Dan to Beer-sheba knew that Samuel was established as a prophet of the Lord'' (I Samuel 3:19-20).

There is one theme which is of the first importance during the whole era of the judges, of Samuel, of Saul and up to David. Put in the form of a question this theme may be stated as follows: Should there be a king in Israel? The problem during that period of the judges was that "there was no king in Israel; every man did what was right in his own eyes" (Judges 21:25). Things went up and down in accordance with the Deuteronomic success formula.

An important exchange took place between the people of God and one judge, Gideon. After Gideon and his men had freed Israel from their enemies the men of Israel came to Gideon and said, "Rule over us, you and your son and your grandson also; for you have delivered us out of the hand of Midian" (Judges 8:22). But in response Gideon said to them: "I will not rule over you, and my son will not rule over you; the Lord will rule over you" (Judges 8:23).

At this juncture in the sacred history of the people of God the whole question of Lordship takes on a new dimension. If there is to be a king in Israel, then the people of God would give their ultimate allegiance to him. But if they did that, then how could God be Lord of their lives? As Jesus was later to say, "No one can serve two masters" (Matthew 6:24).

We have here the problem of divided loyalties, of serving God and the state, of having more than one authority in our lives. And if we do have more than one authority, then there can be no one Lord of our histories.

The elders of Israel came also to Samuel: "Behold, you are old . . . ; now appoint for us a king to govern us" (I Samuel 8:5). Samuel gave voice to the same problem as we have raised, and more dimensions of the problem come out in the request of Israel to him and in his response to it. Israel wanted a king so that they could be "like all the nations" (I Samuel 8:5). They did not want to give exclusive and ultimate allegiance to God as *the* Lord of their histories. They wanted to serve two masters.

And God told the truth to Samuel, who prayed to him for guidance: "They have not rejected you, but they have rejected me from being king over them" (I Samuel 8:7). There cannot be more than one king over us. "Now then, hearken to their voice; only, you shall solemnly warn them, and show them the ways of the king who shall reign over them" (I Samuel 8:9).

And the faithful Samuel does solemnly warn the people, indicating in effect yet another dimension of the problem: when a man is chosen king he will himself cease to take God in Christ as Lord of his history, and towards the people he will act in such a way that they will not do so either (I Samuel 8:10-18).

As we might expect from our own experience "the people" refused to listen to the voice of Samuel; and they said, "No! but we will have a king over us, that we also may be like all the nations, and that our king may govern us and go out before us and fight our battles" (I Samuel 8:19-20). "And the Lord said to Samuel, 'Hearken to their voice, and make them a king' " (I Samuel 8:22).

Samuel anointed Saul king, and the spirit of God was on Saul, and when it was he did mighty deeds in battle against the Philistines and other enemies (I Samuel 9-10). Eventually, however, the spirit of God came upon David, and while Saul slew his thousands, David slew his ten thousands (See I Samuel 18:7).

Samuel, in his farewell address to the people, voiced well the problem of there being a king in Israel and gives us the solution to the problem of divided loyalties, reminding us what it really is to have God in Christ as Lord. "Behold, I have hearkened to your voice . . . and have made a king over you" (I Samuel 12:1). "If you will fear the Lord and serve him and hearken to his voice and not rebel against the commandment of the Lord, and if both you and the king who reigns over you will follow the Lord your God, it will be well; but if you will not hearken to the voice of the Lord, but rebel against the commandment of the Lord, then the hand of the Lord will be against you and your king" (I Samuel 12:14-15).

C. The Moment of David

In David we see the solution of the problem of the people of God serving two masters, the king of Israel and the Lord God. To see this solution it needs to be shown how David became king and how the Bible presents him in his relation to the Lord God.

Saul, king of Israel, did not obey the Lord God in his leadership of the people against the Amalekites (I Samuel 15). "The word of the Lord came to Samuel: 'I repent that I have made Saul king; for he has turned back from following me, and has not performed my commandments' " (I Samuel 15:10-11). And Samuel said to Saul: "Because you have rejected the word of the Lord, he has also rejected you from being king" (I Samuel 15:23).

The Lord sent Samuel to Jesse, the Bethlehemite, "for I have provided for myself a king among his sons" (I Samuel 16:1). And Samuel went and saw the sons, even the youngest, David, who "was ruddy, and had beautiful eyes, and was handsome. And the Lord said, 'Arise, anoint him; for this is he' " (I Samuel 16:12). It was David upon whom the spirit of God was to come with a mighty hand. It was he who was to unite Israel, when he became king.

David entered the service of Saul, the king, and in I Samuel, Chapter 17 he fought Goliath, the giant champion of the Philistines. In this story there are reflected some of the characteristics of the Davidic moment in the sacred historical story.

David came to where the army of Israel under Saul was encamped, intending to bring food for his brothers who were soldiers in the army. After he arrived, Goliath, the Philistine of Gath, challenged the men of Israel. To David, the ruddy youth, all that was important was that this was an affront to the people of God. "Who is this uncircumcised Philistine, that he should defy the armies of the living God?" (I Samuel 17:26).

With no thought at all for himself, David went to Saul: "Let no man's heart fail because of him; your servant will go and fight with this Philistine" (I Samuel 17:32). Saul noted that David was but a boy. But David, in complete trust in God, told how he had killed both lions and bears in defense of his father's flocks. "The Lord God who delivered me from the paw of the lion and from the paw of the bear, will deliver me from the hand of this Philistine" (I Samuel 17:37).

Saul told David to go forth with the Lord's blessing. David refused Saul's armor, for he was not used to such large and heavy pieces. He took what he was used to: his sling and five smooth stones. What he needed, all he needed was his natural God-given talents. He came "in the name of the Lord of hosts, the God of the armies of Israel" (I Samuel 17:45), and that was completely sufficient for him. In that moment God in Christ was his Lord. He simply wanted all the two assembled armies to know, he wanted "all the earth" to know, that "the battle is the Lord's'' (I Samuel 17:46,47).

In the name of the Lord God, David slew Goliath, the Philistine giant champion of Gath. And the spirit of God came upon David again and again, such that the people praised David more than king Saul: "Saul has slain his thousand, and David his ten thousands'' (I Samuel 18:7).

From the Bible and from our knowledge of general history let us see what David did accomplish as king of Israel. He first ruled from Hebron. Then he captured Jerusalem, an independent city, centralizing his authority there. Jerusalem then became the city of David. David converted it to a religious center, a central sanctuary, not in the territory of any one of the twelve tribes of Israel. Jerusalem was a wise choice, because it was a neutral site (See II Samuel 5:6-10; Chronicles 10:4-9).

When he had brought the Ark of the Covenant to Jerusalem (II Samuel 6; I Chronicles 13), and when he had established Jerusalem as his center of political power, he had in fact achieved the unity of the people of God. Under David the people, whom God had delivered out of Egypt, had finally become one. Nathan, the prophet, told David, "Go, do all that is in your heart; for the Lord is with you'' (II Samuel 7:3).

God made his promise to David (See II Samuel 7:8-16). David, the holy man, the king, the man for whom God in Christ is Lord, said this: "Whom am I, O Lord God, and what is my house, that thou hast brought me thus far? . . . Thou art great, O Lord God; for there is none like thee. . . . Now therefore may it please thee to bless the house of thy servant, that it may continue for ever before thee.'' (II Samuel 7:18-29). "So David reigned over all Israel; and David administered justice and equity to all his people'' (II Samuel 8:15).

Some practical ways this unity was achieved by David were that he took the first census (II Samuel 24:2-9; I Chronicles 21). On the basis of this he started a system of military conscription, and also a system of taxation. Under David a bureaucracy developed. Since this sort of thing was new in Israel, David had to draw on personnel from Canaanite city states and on the system of administration of the government of Egypt. Since education is a basic requirement for building up an administrative system there is reason to think that there was also in Israel the formation of a system of schools.[2] Also there were forced labor camps (II Samuel 24).

The international situation favored the establishment of David's empire. Egypt to the south and Assyria to the north were both weak during David's time. David had authority over the whole Holy Land with a network of roads and trade along the highways.

What all this general history means in the sacred history of God's people is simply this: under David the people of God finally become one people. The mark of the Davidic moment is unity, and, since it has been unity of one people under God that has been longed for, then this moment under David must be seen as a time of successful achievement of a goal.

And the momentous character of this sacred historical season of the spirit should not be passed over too quickly. We have suffered in bondage, slaves in an oppressive system, separated from the Lord God. Then in what seems to us to be a mighty act the Lord frees us. He brings us out of bondage. He frees us to give ultimate allegiance to him. But we cannot do this absolutely and without guidelines. We are lost in a kind of absolute freedom wilderness. We are divided among ourselves, and we squabble, complain and murmur. God, in his wisdom, lays down the law for us, to help us find our way out of the fog of our own spiritual wilderness. But we suffer from our own faithlessness, our own inability to follow that law.

And we do not escape the judgment of God, and so we are destined to live out the consequences of our unfaithfulness by wandering further in our wilderness. But God does not fail on his promises. He has said that he will bring us into a land, and we long for that Promised Land. When he leads us into it, however, our evil imagination again controls our lives and we act like spiritual children. Things do not go well for us, so we cry out to the Lord, who raises a champion to deliver us out of our trouble. The judge does just that, and we again acknowledge God as Lord in our lives. But when the dust settles after our salvation we again fall back to our ways of unfaithfulness, our ways of life which acknowledge ourselves as little gods. So things do not go well for us again, and so the cycle continues.

In our confusion and immaturity we long for a king who will always be there to fight our battles for us. The inspired voice of Samuel warns us of the ways of a king, but we hearken not to God's prophet.

But now in David God has brought us not only a king who can and does deliver us from our troubles, but who also is the man among us who himself acknowledges most fully the Lordship of God. The effect of this is to unite the people. God had promised Abraham a great nation, and that nation has been successfully achieved under David the king. This at long last is the nation by whom all the nations can be blessed. This at long last is a nation peacefully and freely united in service to the Lord God under his anointed King David. David is the mighty ruler, the holy man, all in one.

The effect of this comes out in the Bible in II Samuel, Chapter 7. God will make of David a house or dynasty to last forever. King David is anointed by the prophet of God with holy oil. King David is considered the divine son of God, who has a special filial relationship with God. The day of anointing is a day of rebirth and renewal. In Psalm 2:8 the king is promised universal dominion and rulership over all the nations, this being a restatement of God's promise to Abraham in Genesis Chapter 12, that "by you all the families of the earth shall bless themselves."

Jerusalem, the City of David, became the dwelling place of God. It became Zion, the city on the hill, which was a light to all nations. David was the "shoot from the stump of Jesse (Isaiah 11:1), his father. David was an ancestor of Jesus of Nazareth (Matthew 1:1-17). Jesus the Christ was expected to re-establish the reign of David. On that "Palm Sunday," in which Jesus came on the colt from Bethpage and Bethany at the mount of Olives to Jerusalem, the people cried, "Blessed be the kingdom of our father David that is coming! Hosanna in the highest!" (Mark 11:10).

Just as Abraham was not always Abrahamic, so David was not always Davidic. David fell from his status of the holy man of God's people. In this the Bible reminds us graphically again of the fact that it is he who is Lord of history, not we ourselves. David, like us, was an ordinary man, who had ordinary temptations and problems, and who, like us, succumbs to them.

This is told in the annals of the history of the court life of David in II Samuel, from Chapter 9. David's sin was against Uriah, who was fighting for

Israel. One day David "saw . . . a woman bathing; and the woman was very beautiful" (II Samuel 11:2). He inquired about her. He had her brought to his house, and "he lay with her. . . . And the woman conceived: and she sent and told David, 'I am with child' " (I Samuel 11:4-5).

David sent for her husband, Uriah, giving him a present and inviting him to go to his own house and sleep with his own wife. Uriah did not do this, saying that his fellow soldiers could do no such thing. David tried to overcome Uriah's resistance by making him drunk. "But all his plans were foiled by Uriah's reverence for the taboo which forbade sexual intercourse to warriors who had been consecrated for battle" (I Samuel 21:4).[2] After all this he had Uriah sent back to battle and put "in the forefront of the hardest fighting." He saw to it that Uriah's fellow soldiers would draw "back from him, that he may be struck down, and die" (II Samuel 11:15). Uriah was slain. When he heard this, David sent for the widow "and brought her to his house, and she became his wife, and bore him a son" (II Samuel 11:27).

David's actions displeased the Lord; and the Lord sent Nathan, the prophet, to tell David of his sin in the form of a parable. Upon hearing the story David grew angry and said, "As the Lord lives, the man who has done this deserves to die" (II Samuel 12:5).

The true repentence of David as told in II Samuel shows us just how faithful David was. It is one of the ironies of our sacred history how the greatest of saints think that they are the greatest of sinners. The outpourings of David's true faith are seen over and over again. Many of the "Psalms of David" are confessional testimonies of a saint.

The last words of David in II Samuel show David's true faithfulness.

> The Spirit of the Lord speaks by me, his word is upon my tongue. The God of Israel has spoken, the Rock of Israel has said to me: When one rules justly over men, ruling in the fear of God, he dawns on them like the morning light, like the sun shining forth upon a cloudless morning, like rain that makes grass to sprout from the earth. Yea, does not my house stand so with God? For he has made with me an everlasting covenant, ordered in all things and secure. For will he not cause to prosper all my help and my desire? But godless men are all like thorns that are thrown away; for they cannot be taken with the hand; but the man who touches them arms himself with iron and the shaft of a spear, and they are utterly consumed with fire (II Samuel 23:2-7).

After Solomon was anointed king (I Kings 32—48), David charged Solomon, and this charge of his father also reflects David's true faith.

D. The Moment of the Prophets: Isaiah

After the time of David there was the division of the kingdom, which occurred under Solomon, the son of David and Bathsheba. Generally, from the tenth century B.C. onward until the fall of Jerusalem in 587 B.C., the life of the people of God in the southern kingdom of Judah was lived under the threat of extinction by powerful enemies: Egypt to the south, the Assyrians to the north, and, finally the conquering Babylonians to the east. In the sacred historical story this means that the prophets lived during a time when the threat of being conquered was real. The backs of the people of God were to the wall.

Generally, a prophet is one who perhaps foretells the future, but mainly he is one who speaks the word of the Lord. In the 9th and 8th centuries several prophets appeared in society and pronounced judgment upon Israel, judgment on every facet of its life, social, political and individual. Whoever looks to the prophets to support the view that a man of God should not concern himself with judgments on social or political issues will not be satisfied. In the 9th century there are the prophets Elijah and Elisha, and in the 8th century the prophets Amos and Hosea.

During these times the threats to the faith of the people of God became real under, for example, Ahab and Jezebel. Baalism, as a religion of the Canaanites, was widely practiced, and there were great temptations on the people of God to follow such religious practices. The prophets spoke against these manifest temptations.

During this period economic and social developments led to the power of the monarch, the officials of the state, and the military leaders. There was widespread oppression of the people and the prophets clearly sided with the oppressed.

Also there was during this period a resurgence of power in Assyria. The problem posed by this turn of events is how we can square the existence of a powerful foreign aggressor with the belief that the Lord God is in control of all history. In part the answer of the prophets was this: the threat of the Assyrians was an expression of the judgment of God, and in this sense the prophets were saying that God was on the side of the enemy. The answer to the threat of enemies is repentence and true belief. Then the Deuteronomic success formula can be applied.

We have here the idea that true faith is better a child of life under the threat of extinction than it is an offspring of times of success and prosperity. It is true that the Davidic moment is a time of unity and success, and true faith. But too much of that is a dangerous thing, as we saw in the life of David himself. Perhaps the long history from the breakup of the Davidic empire to the fall of Jerusalem, the City of David, to the coming of Christ exists in the sacred historical story to show us that the temptations towards unfaithfulness in times of unity and success are great, the road to recovery of true faithfulness, after such a long period, is itself long and difficult, so difficult that on it we meet with virtual yet not complete extinction of our faith in the fall of Jerusalem and in the exile.

But even along this long and difficult road God is with us still, and with the return of the faithful remnant and the struggle to rebuild what we had before, we are finally ready to accept the savior, to accept the fact that our salvation must come entirely apart from our own efforts to succeed.

In this section there is one prophet that we will consider, namely Isaiah. Briefly, the specific historical situation of Isaiah is this. He lived during the time of King Uzziah, who reigned in the South, in Judah from 783—742 B.C. Jeroboam II was king of the Northern Kingdom of Israel. "Under Uzziah, Judah reached the very peak of her economic and military power." The brief report in II Kings 15:1-7, supplemented by the longer account in II Chronicles 26, gives us a picture of Uzziah's extraordinary accomplishments: the modernization of the army; his conquests in the Philistine plain, which put him in control of the main commercial highways; his commercial expansion into Arabia; his reconstruction of the trade-route seaport city of Elath (formerly Ezion-geber); and his development of agriculture, for, we are told "he loved the soil."[3]

Isaiah came to be a prophet in 742 B.C., "in the year that King Uzziah died" (Isaiah 6:1). His career lasted more than forty years. During this career there were three major historical events. In 735 B.C. the armies of Syria and North Israel invaded Judean soil to force Judah to enter a coalition to stop the Assyrians. This was a futile attempt, since the Assyrian commander Tiglath-pileser conquered Syria in 733-732 B.C. Secondly, the successor to Tiglath-pileser, Shalmansser V, came from Palestine and laid siege to Samaria, the capital of the Northern Kingdom. This occurred in 722-621 B.C. Both of these events greatly troubled Judah. At the end of the eighth century B.C., in 711, another anti-Assyrian revolt was squashed, and in 701, yet another was put down, this requiring an invasion of Sennacherib from Assyria into the Judean territory.[4] Indeed, Isaiah prophesied the word of the Lord in perilous times.

Themes of Isaiah's vision are elaborated in the early chapters of the book of Isaiah. The book which I refer to, the writings of the 8th century prophet, for our purposes is as follows: Isaiah Chapters 1 through 23 and Chapters 36 through 39, which refer to events from the latter years of Isaiah's ministry, are modifications of II Kings 18:13—20:19. It is thought that Chapters 24 through 27, the "little apocalypse," and 34 through 35 and 40 through 66 all belong to later periods than that of the eighth century prophet.

Isaiah sets his theme in Chapter One:

> Come now, let us reason together says the Lord; though your sins are like scarlet, they shall be as white as snow; though they are red like crimson, they shall become like wool. If you are obedient, you shall eat the good of the land; But if you refuse and rebel, you shall be devoured by the sword; for the mouth of the Lord has spoken (Isaiah 1:18-20).

There is hope, if we are willing and obedient:

> And I will restore you judges as the first, and your counselors as at the beginning. Afterward you shall be called the city of righteousness, the faithful city.

> Zion shall be redeemed by justice, and those in her who repent, by righteousness (Isaiah 1:26-27).

But as for the ones who are not faithful:

> But rebels and sinners shall be destroyed together, and those who forsake the Lord shall be consumed (Isaiah 1:28).

> The Lord's day will not be light but darkness, because of the unfaithful (See Isaiah 2:6-21).

> And the haughtiness of man shall be humbled and the pride of men shall be brought low; and the Lord alone will be exalted in that day (Isaiah 2:17).

> The Lord has taken his place to contend, he stands to judge his people. The Lord enters into judgment with the elders and princes of his people: 'It is you who have devoured the vineyard, the spoil of the poor is in your houses. What do you

mean by crushing my people, by grinding the face of the poor?' says the Lord God of hosts (Isaiah 3:13-15).

Isaiah's call to prophesy, or as we might say, to the ministry, is given in Chapter 6 (Isaiah 6:1-8). In this call we learn more of what it is to have God in Christ as Lord. In this account we have one of the clearest accounts of the dynamic movement of the spirit in the sacred history of man in his relation to God.

"In the year that King Uzziah died" the nation was in a state of shock. What would it mean now to the kingdom of Judah in the city of David that their great and faithful leader Uzziah had died? Small wonder that it was in such a time of shock that Isaiah was in the temple. He was continuing to perform his regular duties as priest.

And when he entered the temple on this occasion he met the Lord God "sitting upon a throne, high and lifted up; and his train filled the temple" (Isaiah 6:1). The seraphim called out, "Holy holy holy is the Lord of hosts; the whole earth is full of his glory" (Isaiah 6:3).

This is the Holy One whom Isaiah is meeting, the same one whom Moses met on the mountain of God, the same one who is present yet hidden, present yet "high and lifted up," present yet fearsome and awful. And in the presence of the Holy One there is a shaking of the foundations. Imagine Isaiah's fear, imagine our own fear: "And the foundations of the thresholds shook at the voice of him who called" (Isaiah 6:4).

We, like Isaiah, cannot see this Holy One before whom our very foundations shake. And the house is filled with smoke. In "fear and trembling" we stand before the Holy One. What is our reaction? It would be much like Isaiah's. "Woe is me! For I am lost; for I am a man of unclean lips, and I dwell in the midst of a people of unclean lips; for my eyes have seen the King, the Lord of hosts!" (Isaiah 6:5).

In the presence of the Holy One we are undone, and we realize how much we are lost, how much we have fallen short in faithfulness. But one cannot realize this until one comes into the presence of the Lord, high and lifted up, the Holy One, the foundations shake, and we are in awe. We know our uncleanness and our shortcomings. We say, "Woe is me." But in our confession we know God's forgiveness, as did Isaiah: "Behold . . . your guilt is taken away, your sin forgiven" (Isaiah 6:7).

We cannot know the unburdening feeling of being forgiven until we have confessed our unfaithfulness, and we cannot confess our unfaithfulness until we realize that we are lost and undone, and we cannot realize that we are lost and undone until we come into the presence of the Holy One, high and lifted up. There is a dynamic movement of the spirit here in the calling of Isaiah in this crucial moment in the sacred historical story.

With the unburdening of the soul, then it is that we receive the call and feel the compulsion to go out into our worlds and to tell of what we have found in the presence of the Lord. "And I heard the voice of the Lord saying, 'Whom shall I send, and who will go for us?' Then I said, 'Here am I! Send me' " (Isaiah 6:8).

What Isaiah did declare was that we are to trust in the Lord, with quiet and calm. "For thus said the Lord God, the Holy One of Israel, 'In returning and rest you shall be saved; in quietness and in trust shall be your strength' " (Isaiah 30:15). We wait and we believe. "If you will not believe, surely you shall not be established" (Isaiah 7:9).

Never is the hand of judgment far from Isaiah's lips. "Because this people have refused the waters of Shiloah that flow gently, . . . therefore, behold, the Lord is bringing up against them the waters of the River, mighty and many, the king of Assyria and all his glory; and it will rise over all its channels and go over all its banks; and it will sweep on into Judah, it will overflow and pass on, reaching even to the neck; and its outspread wings will fill the breadth of your land, O Immanu-el" (Isaiah 8:6-8).

Nevertheless there is hope. "Bind up the testimony, seal the teaching among my disciples. I will wait for the Lord, who is hiding his face from the house of Jacob, and I will hope in him" (Isaiah 8:16,17).

What we, who have God in Christ as Lord, are to do is to wait on the Lord in quietness and trust. It is he who is guiding us, he who has for us the authoritative work. It is he who gives us the power to act in accordance with his purposes, no matter how much resourcefulness it requires.

We wait upon the Lord and trust that no matter what our situation is, no matter if we walk in the valley of the shadow of death, no matter if we, like Abraham, are called upon to sacrifice everything, we wait still upon the Lord. We trust that somehow, we know not how, his promises will be fulfilled. We can be at peace when we wait upon the Lord. To borrow from the "little apocalypse," we may quote the following: "Thou dost keep him in perfect peace, whose mind is stayed on thee, because he trusts in thee. Trust in the Lord for ever, for the Lord God is an everlasting rock" (Isaiah 26:3-4).

Trust in the Lord will allow the faithful to survive no matter how difficult things become, no matter how broad the judgment on those who look only to the power of the nations and the king. "Therefore thus says the Lord God, 'Behold, I am laying in Zion for a foundation a stone, a tested stone, a precious cornerstone, of a sure foundation: 'He who believes will not be in haste' '' (Isaiah 28:16). There will be a faithful remnant, and there will continue to be a Jerusalem. It will be delivered, "for out of Jerusalem shall go forth a remnant, and out of Mount Zion a band of survivors. The zeal of the Lord of hosts will accomplish this. Therefore thus says the Lord concerning the king of Assyria: He shall not come into this city, or shoot an arrow there, or come before it with a shield, or cast up a siege-mound against it. By the way that he came, by the same he shall return, and he shall not come into this city, says the Lord. For I will defend this city to save it, for my own sake and for the sake of my servant David" (Isaiah 37:32-35).

There are certain passages in Isaiah which speak of the coming role of Zion in the future life of the world of nations.

> It shall come to pass in the latter days that the mountain of the house of the Lord shall be established as the highest of the mountains, and shall be raised above the hills; and all the na-tions shall flow to it, and many peoples shall come, and say: 'Come, let us go up to the mountain of the Lord, to the house of Jacob; that he may teach us his ways and that we may walk in his paths.' For out of Zion shall go forth the law, and the word of the Lord from Jerusalem. He shall judge between the nations, and shall decide for many peoples and they shall beat their swords into plowshares, and their spears into pruning hooks; nation shall not lift up sword against nation, neither shall they learn war any more (Isaiah 2:2-4).

> And he said, 'Hear then, O house of David. Is it too little for you to weary men, that you weary my God also? Therefore, the Lord himself will give you a sign. Behold, a young woman shall conceive and bear a son, and shall call his name Immanuel' (Isaiah 7:13-14).

Isaiah prophesies the coming of the savior, the coming role of Zion, which is to be carried out in the image of what David was in Israel. "There shall come forth a shoot from the stump of Jesse . . . and the spirit of the Lord shall rest upon him . . ." (Isaiah 11:1-2).

> For to us a child is born, to us a son is given; and the government will be upon his shoulder and his name will be called 'Wonderful Counselor, Mighty God, Everlasting Father, Prince of Peace.' Of the increase of his government and of peace there will be no end, upon the throne of David, and over his kingdom, to establish it, and to uphold it with justice and with righteousness from this time forth and forevermore. The zeal of the Lord of hosts will do this (Isaiah 9:6-7).

E. The Moments of the Destruction of the Temple, the "Loss" of the Davidic Line and the Fall of Jerusalem

The people of God, first, however, had to face the worst possible situation imaginable, the combined events of the fall of Jerusalem, the destruction of the temple and the apparent loss of the Davidic line.

There had been in Judah a religious revival and a revival of nationalism under Josiah, the king (See II Kings 23). There was, under this effective and faithful king, what may be called a Deuteronomic reformation. The "book of the covenant" which had been found in the house of the Lord was, we think, the book of Deuteronomy, and the reformation was carried out in accordance with it.

Josiah died in 609 B.C., and following this, Egypt took over Palestine. In 605 B.C. the Egyptian control over Palestine was broken when the Babylonian Nebuchadnezzar routed the Egyptian army."[5]

Josiah was succeeded by Jehoiakim, who became a vassal to Babylon (II Kings 24:1). But in 598 B.C. Jehoiakim refused to pay tribute, rebelling against the king of Babylon. Jehoiakim had been inspired by the nationalist spirit born under Josiah, but the Lord was not with Jehoiakim, for he sent against him enemies to destroy him (See II Kings 24:2-5).

Jehoiakim was succeeded by Jehoiachin (II Kings 24:8). Under his brief reign "the Babylonian army laid siege to Jerusalem and seized the city on March 16, 597 B.C."[6] Then was an exile of the leading Judean citizens to Babylon, and this is described in II Kings 24:12-16. Jehoiachin himself was carried away to Babylon. "And the king of Babylon made Mattaniah, Jehoiachin's uncle, king in his stead, and changed his name to Zedekiah" (II Kings 24:17). The significance of this act is that Nebuchadnezzar not only spared the city of David, but he allowed the Davidic family to continue its rule.

But Zedekiah soon rebelled against Babylon. Consequently, Jerusalem came under siege for two years and it was conquered in 587 B.C. "The temple and the town were looted and burned, the walls of the city were pulled down, large elements of the population were exiled, and the state was incorporated into the Babylonian provincial system, with a governor appointed to administer the area (II Kings 25:8-22)."[7]

A significant passage closes II Kings.

> And in the thirty-seventh year of the exile of Jehoiachin king of Judah, in the twelfth month, on the twenty-seventh day of the month, Evil-merodach king of Babylon, in the year that he began to reign, graciously freed Jehoiachin King of Judah from prison; and he spoke kindly to him, and gave him a seat above the seats of the kings who were with him in Babylon. So Jehoiachin put off his prison garments. And every day of his life he dined regularly at the king's table; and for his allowance, a regular allowance was given him by the king, every day a portion, as long as he lived (II Kings 25:27-30).

The significance of this is that during the exile the Davidic line was preserved. Small consolation this, however, since it was not preserved in Jerusalem, the City of David, from whom a savior would come as a "shoot from the stump of Jesse."

In the sacred history of the people of God this was the lowest of the lowest moments of all. This was the moment when all seemed hopeless. It had been prophesied that the savior was to come from the city of David, but now Jerusalem was in dust and ashes. For the Biblical Christian it is often said that there is no such thing as ultimate despair. God is always with us, and so there is always hope. Now, Jerusalem is in ashes. What hope can there be?

We believe, however, that God is with us even though we can see no hope. God is preparing us to receive the savior who is to become our Lord, by reminding us that it is not we who save ourselves. God was with Abraham in his time of trial, when he had nothing to cling to except his faith. God will be with the disciples of Jesus after his crucifixion, when their expectation and hopes that Jesus was the Messiah will have been dashed.

So too, with the fall of Jerusalem, God is with the people, even as we will see in Ezekiel in the valley of the dry bones. And so it is with us in our own personal moments of seeming despair, loneliness and loss of hope. God is with us. In these moments we are not feeling the way we do because God is absent.

What the Biblical Christian is to do is to believe in the promises of God, to believe that God is working out his purposes no matter how he feels. His job is to let God in Christ be his Lord, no matter what.

F. The Maturity of Davidic Success and Its Downside Aftermath

In the mature person it is a mark of practical wisdom to have hopes for life, and to know under what circumstances these hopes are to be realized. In our developing maturity we have known a sense of mission. We have had the perspicacity to discern what that mission is. In our Abrahamic seasons of the spirit in our quest for maturity we have had a sense of promise of the "great nation" for which we seek. A step towards that social state of affairs in our society was taken after the exodus moment of our spirits in the freedom of the people as one and in the new "law" we devised for ourselves and our people.

The conquest and settlement moments are those moments in which the conditions for the fulfillment of this promise are ripe. It is a moment when, we think, we will get beyond the continuous up and down passages from bondage to freedom to bondage which we knew in the wilderness. The time when the long-awaited promise is to be fulfilled is a time when with Brigham Young we say "This is the place," where this "great nation" can be realized.

The place is good, a land or a situation "flowing with milk and honey." We make moves in perhaps a geographical change of location or a professional change of job or career, or a rather radical change in life style. These moves may be swift and successful where we move in and take over. On the other hand they may be slow, rather like an infiltration or a gradual fitting in.

In the quest for maturity there has been the continual passages from bondage to freedom. In the law and second moment in the wilderness we redefined our positions intellectually, emotionally and socially, yet we failed to remain true to our new identification. We were independent, yet we could not be mature enough to remain dependent on that law.

In our settlement, in our new situation, we may have expected quick results, quick realization of hopes long held, but such unrealistic expectations may be frustrated. On the other hand one may come to a place with the realization that this is the place for him. We may for a time, simply win it over, not entirely by our own doing, but by the rightness of this place and time for us.

The conquest and settlement moments in the life searching for maturity are times of rejoicing and renewing of our hopes. It is a time when we might well have renewal ceremonies in which we remember from whence we have come and we renew ourselves in the settlement in the "land" where all our hopes are to be realized.

Of course, our hopes are not yet realized. In our life in our new region and social situation we may have ups and downs accordingly as things are going well or badly. Our needs for dependencies during these times might well be great, and our emotions and feelings might be unstable and our practical judgments unfounded. For periods of time we might look to those who will lead us, and during their period of leadership we might survive difficulties and even conquer adversaries. We might at these times be led to think that we do not need such leaders, but without them we return to our former instabilities. In our search for maturity we may again follow what, in the sacred historical rehearsal, we called the "Deuteronomic success formula."

During this time of developing maturity in our new region or situation we may long for a permanent leader, a "king," who will show us the way. We have had in the past the practical wisdom to make the necessary judgments about what is best for us in our lives, but we have failed to steer a steady course for ourselves emotionally and socially. In the second moment in the wilderness we knew our failure to follow the course we judged best for us. In the moment of conquest and settlement we went up and down accordingly as we were doing well or poorly in relation to our colleagues, neighbors and adversaries. When we did well we were under the protection and guidance of a strong leader. In this instance we seem to be in an adolescent mode of behavior, one which needs restricting and guiding hands and yet one which thinks they are not necessary.

When we get tired of the instability we cry out for a permanent leader. It is rather like our situation after we were freed from bondage in our Egypt, or state of complete dependence. Now we want a permanent leader just like before we wanted a new set of binding rules and restrictions. In our independent judgment we want dependence. We want this even though in our heart of hearts our "Samuel" will warn us of what this dependence will mean for us. The prophet in this instance tells us that a permanent leader or king will be corrupted in his power. He will tend to view the whole society in terms of his own position and success or failure of his own leadership. He will think of himself first and foremost, and he will tend to take all things unto himself. He will, in effect, exemplify the problems when we fell originally from the true community in the beginning moments of our maturity.

We want a king in spite of the divided loyalties which we will have in this season of our spirits. If we have a permanent leader we will have more than one authority in our lives. We will have our own independent judgment on which to rely, and we also will have the allegiance to the sovereign power over us. If we surrender our wills to the will of the sovereign there will be removed from our shoulders the awesome responsibility of developing our own maturity. We are bound to do this if our "great nation" is to be realized. The leader will supplant our own functions of practical judgment and the steering of a steady course for us. To be sure we still will have the capacity to make such judgments for the best for ourselves. Having surrendered our wills to the sovereign king such judgments will at best be of secondary importance.

That power of the leader in our lives will usher in a period of success and unity. It will be a successful time in that it is a time of the fulfillment of a long-awaited promise, the promise of the "great nation," of a situation or state in life when all our hopes as a people will be realized. Things will go well with us, and we will prosper. It will be a time of unity in that it is a time when we have it all together in ourselves and in our society. In these senses it will resemble the true community in the beginning moments of our quest for maturity.

In the sacred historical story David was the holy man faithful to God, and he was the wise and efficient ruler. In him the problem of divided loyalties was solved in that people could be faithful to God by being faithful to David. In our own lives in which we search for maturity such a Davidic moment will also be a time of success and unity. We will think ourselves mature when we reach a Davidic stage. It will be a time in our mature lives when we display the greatest independence. We will be our own king. In our practical judgments, in our emotional steadiness, in our social regularity we will clearly have the most independence possible.

This will not, however, be a time of the sort of self-sufficiency we had in the moment of Noah. In this current moment we will work independently and also in cooperation with others in the task of building our great society under our successful ruler. We will not know the complete self-sufficiency of a Noah who stood apart from, even opposite to his society in his judgment of condemnation.

Ironically, this Davidic moment, which highlights independence, will also have a dependent, even a self-insufficient side. If we are our own Davidic king we will, like David the faithful holy man, swear allegiance to what we serve and those whom we lead. In our quest for maturity there is also a state in which we are dependent, just as the Old Testament David was dependent on his Lord to whom he, the king, looked for guidance. If the Davidic king is another person or group or institution to whom we have given our allegiance, then we will be dependent on him as on a sovereign leader and self-insufficient before him.

If we are our own king this Davidic time will be a time of self-sufficiency.

This cannot, however, be complete, even for the king himself. For those ruled there can be independent judgments for oneself but the behavior in society will always be subject to the rule of the king. Thus there cannot in this moment be self-sufficiency. There is, as we have seen, a self-insufficiency as we surrender our wills to the sovereign power we call the "king." There is also a dependence both of the ruler to the ruled and the ruled to the success of the king in giving us the stability we lacked in our moments of conquest and settlement. We are dependent on this king for the period of success and unity which we enjoy.

The Davidic moment of kingship is yet another stage in our developing process of becoming mature. The success and unity of this moment is a fragile thing. The distance between kingly self-sufficiency and self-insufficiency is too great. The king may act un-kingly. He may, as we were warned, take all things unto himself. He may fail to judge and act as a king. If we are under the sovereign power of another king we will rebel. If we are king over our own lives we will lose our psychological unity, falling apart in the process.

The fall will be hard in the downside aftermath of the Davidic moment. We will have fallen from the achievement of long-awaited, long-hoped-for success and unity in our lives. This point is a crucial test in our developing maturity. What recourse do we have? We cannot but judge that our situation is not the best for us. We cannot help from feeling the great loss. We cannot look with favor on the breakup of socially constructive behavior.

This will be a crucial time for us, and into our lives will come our prophet, giving us the word for us at this point in our development. He will point out to us that the temptations to fall away from what we know to be best for us are great in our Davidic times of success and unity. He will say that the road to recovery of what we enjoyed is itself long and difficult, so difficult that we may fear for our very existences. He will, however, give us hope that our reconstruction of ourselves and our society after this failure and breakup will be accomplished.

What will be our psychological state during this interim in our quest for maturity? In these dangerous times we may be afraid and the foundations of our security and success may shake. We may say, "Woe is me! For I am lost." We realize that in these Isaiah moments we have fallen far short of the ideal of maturity. We have fallen but to be mature we can live with ourselves during these times. We can go on. We can even face the challenge and say with Isaiah, "Here I am! Send me."

What we have to realize is that there is hope if we are steadfast even in the face of danger. We are to remain true to ourselves. We are to continue to exercise the practical judgments necessary for maturity. The difficulty here lies in the emotions. How can we achieve a steadiness required in the mature life? What this Isaiah moment requires is quietness and trust. In this lies our strength, he tells us. We will have a strong sense of judgment upon ourselves during this time. What is required, however, is simply to wait for the time when the Davidic moment of success and unity will be ours once again. In waiting there is, in itself, a kind of maturity, a steadiness needed for our development.

Waiting in quietness and confidence and strength is very difficult in the aftermath of the breakup of the success and unity of our Davidic moment in our quest for maturity. Such waiting is especially difficult when we have no clear sense of what we can do for ourselves. When there are no practically wise judgments we can make for ourselves except to wait, it is especially difficult to be emotionally mature. It is difficult to be steady in our feelings and our behavior.

In the period of waiting things go from bad to worse in our fall of Jerusalem moments. Our Jerusalem is that place for us where we achieved the success and unity of the Davidic moment. Our Jerusalem is that place or situation where we believe we can recover it again. So far as we know it is the only such place. In the quest for maturity there will be such moments. The forces of the world which threaten us will lay siege to that place wherein all our hopes are to be realized. That place will be "conquered."

The bottom will drop out. The hopes we had realized in our Davidic moment will be shattered. We will not see how they can be realized again. As in the Abrahamic moment in our quest for maturity, these times are times when we do not see how all the promises we have had can possibly be fulfilled. Things now seem hopeless. As we did in our Abrahamic moments, however, we must just go on believing what now seems impossible, hoping that somewhere, somehow we will find that secure rock on which we may stand firmly once again.

7

The Moment of Exile, Return and Reconstruction

A. The Exile Moment

Jerusalem had fallen, the temple had been destroyed, and the Davidic line, although still intact, sat no longer in the City of David. The people were in exile in Babylon, adjusting in their several ways to an entirely new situation.

In the sacred historical story there is, however, no loss of hope for one for whom God in Christ is Lord.

> Comfort, comfort my people says your God. Speak tenderly to Jerusalem, and cry to her that her warfare is ended, that her iniquity is pardoned, that she has received from the Lord's hand double for all her sins.

> A voice cries: 'In the wilderness prepare the way of the Lord, make straight in the desert a highway for our God. Every valley shall be lifted up, and every mountain and hill be made low; the uneven ground shall become level, and the rough places a plain. And the glory of the Lord shall be revealed, and all flesh shall see it together, for the mouth of the Lord has spoken' (Isaiah 40:1-15).

Second Isaiah, which for our purposes refers to Isaiah, Chapters 40 through 66, is the herald of good tidings. The word of the Lord is sure, even though his ways are unknown to us. Of this we may be certain, even in our state of seemingly tragic separation from him. The promises of God will be fulfilled.

> The grass withers, the flower fades; but the word of our God will stand forever (Isaiah 40:8).

> For my thoughts are not your thoughts, neither are your ways my ways, says the Lord. For as the heavens are higher than the earth, so are my ways higher than your ways and my thoughts than your thoughts. For as the rain and the snow come down from heaven, and return not thither but water the earth, making it bring forth and sprout, giving seed to the sower and bread to the eater, so shall my word be that goes forth from my mouth; it shall not return to me empty, but it shall accomplish that which I purpose, and prosper in the thing for which I sent it (Isaiah 55:8-11).

The Lord is active in history, and in history his word "stands forever," in contrast to other historical changing phenomena, the withering of the grass and the fading of the flower.

This, our Lord, is both our creator and redeemer, and he alone is Lord (See Isaiah 40:12-31). For Isaiah, as for the Biblical Christian, the Lord God is the creator of the heavens and the earth. We believe that he redeems his creation. As creator the Lord God is sovereign. There is none like him or beside him.

> Have you not known? Have you not heard? Has it not been told you from the beginning? Have you not understood from the foundations of the earth? It is he who sits above the circle of the earth, and its inhabitants are like grasshoppers; who stretches out the heavens like a curtain, and spread them like a tent to dwell in; who brings princes to naught, and makes the rulers of the earth as nothing (Isaiah 40:21-33).

> To whom then will you compare me, that I should be like him? says the Holy One (Isaiah 40:25).

"The purpose of this appeal to . . . (the Lord's) power as Creator was to comfort Israel, who in the desolation of Babylonian exile was thinking that . . . (the Lord) did not see or care what had happened to his people. There must have been many Jews who watched the procession of the idols in the Babylonian festivals, and all but conceded that Babylonian victory was historical proof that Marduk was king."[1] In this despairing situation the prophet speaks:

> Have you not known? Have you not heard? (The Lord) is the everlasting God, the Creator of the ends of the earth.

> He does not faint or grow weary, his understanding is unsearchable. He gives power to the faint, and to him who has no might he increases strength (Isaiah 40:28-29).

Our belief is that God is creator and Lord. Even the weary exiles should, as we all should, wait expectantly upon the Lord.

> Even youths shall faint and be weary, and young men shall fall exhausted; but they who wait for the Lord shall renew their strength, they shall mount up with wings like eagles, they shall run and not be weary, they shall walk and not faint (Isaiah 40:30-31).

We are powerless at times, as Israel certainly was in the time of Isaiah. They were threatened by powerful international forces. Yet even now in these perilous conditions the faithful Biblical Christian waits upon the Lord God, for his purposes to be fulfilled in history.

There will be a new Exodus, and thus there is hope for a new freedom from exile.

> Awake, awake, put on strength, O arm of the Lord; awake, as in the days of old, the generations of long ago. Was it not thou that didst dry up the sea, the waters of the great deep; that didst make the depths of the sea a way for the redeemed to pass over? And the ransomed of the Lord shall return, and come to Zion with singing, everlasting joy shall be upon their heads; they shall obtain joy and gladness, and sorrow and sighing shall flee away (Isaiah 51:9-11).

There will be a new beginning for the people of God, just as there was a new beginning in the exodus from Egypt.

God is with us, and he will help us.

> For I, the Lord your God, hold your right hand; it is I who say
> to you, 'Fear not, I will help you' (Isaiah 41:13).

Israel, the people of God, are the chosen people, and they shall be a light to all nations. We are the elect, chosen by God with whom we have a covenant.

> And I have put my words in your mouth, and hid you in the
> shadow of my hand, stretching out the heavens and laying the
> foundations of the earth, and saying to Zion, 'You are my
> people' (Isaiah 51:16).

Yet there are no ends or limits to the reach of God. There is an emphasis here on the universality of God's reach, which stands as an echo of God's promise to Abraham, that there would be a nation made of him by whom "all the families of the earth shall bless themselves" (Genesis 12:3).

> Thus says God, the Lord, who created the heavens and
> stretched them out, who spread forth the earth and what
> comes from it, who gives breath to the people upon it:
>
> I am the Lord, I have called you in righteousness, I have taken
> you by the hand and kept you; I have given you as a covenant
> to the people, a light to the nations, to open the eyes that are
> blind, to bring out the prisoners from the dungeon, from the
> prison those who sit in darkness.
>
> I am the Lord, that is my name; my glory I give to no other,
> nor my praise to graven images.
>
> Behold, the former things have come to pass, and new things I
> now declare; before they spring forth I tell you of them (Isaiah
> 42:5-9).
>
> Turn to me and be saved, all the ends of the earth! For I am
> God, and there is no other (Isaiah 45:22).

Here in the scripture in this moment of exile we have the clearest indication of universality of reach. "Those spacious horizons reflect the immense vistas opened to the Jewish people, who had been thrust out of the narrow corridor of Palestine into the larger world . . . . There is a broad universality in Second Isaiah's message and yet never does he surrender the conviction that Israel occupies a special place in . . . (the Lord's) historical plan . . . . The ancient motif of the covenant faith, 'I am your God and you are my people,' runs through all the poems."[2]

It will be by the people of God, most perfectly realized in the moment of David, that the light will be brought to all nations to open the eyes that are blind, to bring out the prisoners from the dungeons, from those who sit in darkness'' (Isaiah 42:7).

There is no other than the Lord God of history who is in control of the history of all peoples and nations. The Lord alone directs the course of history. It is he who is the savior of all men. "Turn to me and be saved, all the ends of the earth. For I am God, and there is no other" (Isaiah 45:22). Those who are not of the people of God, those "who carry about their wooden idols, and keep on praying to a god that cannot save" (Isaiah 45:20), should assemble themselves and turn to the Lord God who is in control of their destinies. "To me every knee shall bow, every tongue shall swear'' (Isaiah 45:23).

For one for whom God in Christ is Lord, the savior will come in the form of a suffering servant.

> Who has believed what we have heard? And to whom has the arm of the Lord been revealed? For he grew up before him like a young plant, and like a root out of dry ground; he had no form or comeliness that we should look at him, and no beauty that we should desire him. He was despised and rejected by men; a man of sorrows and acquainted with grief; and as one from whom men hide their faces he was despised, and we esteemed him not (Isaiah 53:1-3).

There is the question as to who the suffering servant is. One interpretation has it that the Suffering Servant is Israel. In Isaiah 49:3 the Servant is explicitly identified with Israel:

> And he said to me, "You are my servant, Israel, in whom I will be glorified."

(See also Isaiah 41:8-10)

But the servant may also be seen as an individual. In this regard Isaiah 49:1 is crucial.

> Although in this pasage it is emphatically said that the Servant is Israel (verse 3), it is also said that he has a mission *to* Israel, implying a distinction from the covenant community. The Servant affirms that . . . (the Lord) has called him from the womb to gather Israel to . . . (Him). . . . The "I" who speaks appears to be an individual, and this impression is strengthened by the concrete, personal description of "the man of sorrows" in Isaiah 53. So we are confronted with a singular problem: On the one hand, in many cases the similarities between Israel and the Servant are so close as to indicate that they are the same; and, on the other, the differences seem to be so sharp as to indicate that Israel is not the Servant . . . .
>
> Again and again we have seen that in the Old Testament an individual may incarnate the whole community of Israel, or vice versa, the community may be addressed as an individual who stands in direct, personal relation to God . . . .
>
> So it is unnecessary to choose between an individual and a corporate interpretation of the Servant . . . , for both are true to the Israelite sense of community.[3]

In the sacred history of the people of God the moment in exile is a compounding of the hopelessness found in the moment when Jerusalem fell. If there is a sense of hopelessness at the fall of Jerusalem there is even more so now, for the conditions under which there could be a rekindling of hope seem even more remote. We have sunk even deeper into a spiritual season of despair in our sacred historical moment of the exile.

Ironically, it is in this moment that the expressions of faith are filled with the greatest pathos and sense of hope. These are the expressions of faith that we have amply seen in the poems of Second Isaiah.

It is in our moments of deepest and most compounded despair that we know the spiritual need for something steady and sure, something not within ourselves, who are so despairing. In this season of the spirit it is only the Lord God who is steady and sure. The Christian has to let himself go at this point. He has to believe what seems preposterous and even absurd or at least way out of reach. He has to believe that God is still in control despite all appearances to the contrary. He, like Abraham, has to believe the preposterous. Somehow, we know not how, there will be hope. The faith being expressed in this spiritual season of despair comes to this: there is no limit to the reach or power of God, and in this, and in this alone, there is hope.

B. The Moments of Return and Reconstruction

In 539 B.C. Cyrus, King of Persia, conquered Babylon. His expanding domain was to become the Persian Empire, which was to last until the time of Alexander the Great. Referring to his various conquered peoples and territories, Cyrus writes in his *Cylinder* as follows: "I returned to (these) sacred cities on the other side of the Tigris, the sanctuaries of which have been in ruins for a long time, the images which live therein and established for them permanent sanctuaries. I (also) gathered all their (former) inhabitants and returned (to them) their habitations."[4] Cyrus thus issued an edict two versions of which may be found in Ezra 1:2-4 and 3-5. Cyrus appointed Sheshbassar, son of Jehoiachin, to head up the return. The Davidic line was still intact.

We can say that the moment of the return and reconstruction, as a matter of general history, may be divided into four segments. The first was the edict of Cyrus and the freeing of the people from bondage in Babylon.

The second is the return itself under Zerubbabel, a descendant of Jehoichin, and therefore a king in the Davidic line. During this time a beginning was made on the rebuilding of the temple (See Ezra 1:5), an altar was constructed for true worship (See Ezra Chapter three), and the walls of the city were rebuilt.

We need not think that there was a mass exodus from Babylon to Jerusalem. There are lists of those who returned in Ezra, Chapter 2 and Nehemiah, Chapter 7. In Ezra the number is set at 50,000. Actually the migration back to Jerusalem took place over a period of several generations. Many of the Jews had been comfortable in Babylon. They had reason to stay. Not many of us are willing to take an Abrahamic journey, willing to sacrifice much, or everything, just to be faithful to the Lord God. We do, however, find a community in Jerusalem. We call this "the faithful remnant." Over this remnant Zerubbabel was the chief civil authority.

During this period the altar was built, as one of the first acts of the people, but also there was the installation of the Levites or priests. There was at least the laying of the foundations of a new temple. In 515 B.C. the temple was finished. The leadership of the community was now vested in the High Priest, Joshua, and his successors, and henceforth, Israel was to be a temple-centered community.

The third segment of the return and reconstruction is a reconstruction under Nehemiah. Nehemiah arrived in 445 B.C. during the height of the Persian Empire. Under him there were introduced stiff policies of exclusivism, policies which clearly defined what it is to be a Jew. According to his reforms, the first of the two standards was birth in a Jewish family, where both mother and father were Jewish, and what was even better, where there was a long line of Jewish descendants. Nehemiah strictly prohibited intermarriage. (See Nehemiah Chapter 13; see also the same emphasis in Ezra, Chapters 9 and 10.) The second of these two standards was loyalty to the Torah and the faithful support of the Temple. There was to be a strict adherence to the law, especially the law of the Sabbath.

The fourth segment of the return and reconstruction concerns the work of Ezra, who may be called the father of Judaism. Ezra, a priest, came from Babylon to conduct services of worship. He brought with him the book of the Law of Moses. In Nehemiah the people gathered to hear Ezra's book of the law (Nehemiah 8:1-8). There was a reading of the law, then a celebration of the Feast of Tabernacles according to the direction of the Law (See Leviticus 23:42-43); then there was a covenant renewal ceremony. (See Nehemiah Chapter 9). The people confessed their sins, and Ezra offered a prayer on the part of the people. The book of the law probably was the Pentateuch as edited by the priests during the exile in Babylon.

In this segment there is another of the many rehearsals of the sacred history, which, as in this case, often occur in covenant-renewal ceremonies. As has been evident throughout the rehearsal the very stuff of Israel's faith lies in such rehearsals. In a helpful way Bernard Anderson outlines the "salient aspects of the prayer" of Ezra in this covenant renewal ceremony.

1 . Yahweh, the only God, is creator and sustainer of all that is (verse 6).
2 . He called Abraham out of Ur of Babylonia and promised to give his descendants an inheritance in Canaan (vss. 7-8).
3 . When Israel was oppressed in Egypt, Yahweh kept his promise. He manifested his presence in their midst by various signs and wonders, and by giving the Law to Moses on Mount Sinai (vss. 9-15).
4 . In spite of Israel's incapacity for faith, Yahweh showed himself as "a God ready to forgive, gracious and merciful, slow to anger and abounding in steadfast love." Rebellious Israel was sustained in the wilderness by divine grace (vss. 16-21).
5 . Yahweh gave Israel kingdoms and peoples, and brought them victoriously into Canaan. Thus the people prospered and increased (vss. 22-25).
6 . Nevertheless, Israel continued to be rebellious. So Yahweh disciplined his people, raising up prophets to warn them and giving the people into the hand of enemies when they refused to listen. However, Yahweh graciously spared a remnant (vss. 26-31).
7 . Especially since the time of the kings of Assyria, the hardships have been grievous. Yet Yahweh has been just in all these events. He has been faithful; the people have been unfaithful (vss. 32-54).
8 . Because of their sins the people are now slaves (i.e. vassals of Persia) in the very land that Yahweh gave them, and its rich yield is taken away by heavy taxation (vss. 35-37).[5]

In the sacred history of the people of God the return and reconstruction is a moment of the rekindling of hope. This sacred historical moment represents the creation of all the conditions necessary for the savior to arise. The faithful remnant have acted in faithfulness, expressing, like Abraham, the willingness to go out from Babylon, where they had gained some security, to go back to Jerusalem, which still lay in dust and ashes. Now with the city, altar and temple rebuilt and with right worship instituted, the people are ready for the savior to come. Yet, as Ezra reminds us all, we are still in bondage. This happens over and over again in the sacred historical story. We are in bondage, slaves in the Persian empire. It matters not whether we are bound to Egypt, or to Persia or to the many restrictions which bind us in our contemporary lives as individuals or as a nation. We are bound, we are ready for a new exodus as prophesied by Second Isaiah. This will come, we believe, in Jesus the Christ.

C. The Maturity of Hopelessness and Recovery of Hope

Things will go from worse to almost unbearable in the moment of exile in our search for maturity. This moment of exile in our lives is the period of complete self-insufficiency. It is the moment which we cannot find anything in ourselves to locate our hope. In our fall of Jerusalem season of hopelessness what we had built up had been lost. Now the hopelessness is compounded, for we have been removed from the scene where our hopes might possibly again be realized. We have become subject to forces beyond our control.

In this season of the spirit the person questing for maturity has to let himself be utterly dependent on whatever constancies there are in his life outside of himself. In his practical judgment he understands that there is simply nothing he can or ought to do to better his situation. In his emotional life he has a frightening, empty, meaningless feeling of impotence. Thus is his intellectual and emotional self-sufficiency.

There can be no independence, certainly no self-sufficiency, in this hour. The promise, the hope, the direction he had known in former moments has now been lost. Properly speaking he is not even dependent. This is a radical dependence or self-insufficiency to the extreme.

It is only to his social life to which he can turn for any constancy. He can be a "suffering servant" to those close to him. With loved ones, family, friends or associates he can simply do one thing after another. He can simply do what circumstances outside himself require him to do. In this there is a kind of social steadiness. It is not one based on independent intellectual judgment. It is not one based on a positive emotional attitude. It is one based on nothing but the doing of what seems required, one thing after the other.

Ironically during this "dark night of the soul" there will come forth expressions of hope. Even as "the grass withers and the flower fades" there will come forth something from deep inside himself which is a rock which seems like it will stand forever. In spite of everything there will be a hope that there will again, after this time of hopelessness, be the exercise of independent practical judgment for the best for himself, that again there will be positive feelings, and meaningful social steadiness. There will, somehow, we know not how, be a new exodus from the current hopeless state of bondage, a new beginning of freedom and independence in our lives.

Such a new beginning comes in our moments of return and reconstruction. Because of circumstances not under our voluntary control we will again be able to see and return to the locus of our hopes, our Jerusalem. This is the place or situation where we can begin to rebuild our lives. Our hopes during this moment will be rekindled. There will have been the new exodus for which we have longed even in our darkest, most hopeless hour.

During the reconstruction of our lives there will be new rules and laws to live by, new definitions of social maturity. We will again be able to make practical judgments about how best to follow these rules. We will again feel the tremendous hope and longing for the return of what we once had but lost in the Davidic moment in our search for maturity. Now, perhaps, we are prepared for it.

In the return and reconstruction moments in our developing maturity the emphasis will be on independence. The return itself is a risk, an Abrahamic journey taken without explicit knowledge of what it will be like when we get back to our Jerusalem. As also was the case in our Abrahamic moment, the journey involves at least a willingness to sacrifice what we might have achieved in our moments of exile. We had become used to our place of exile. Now the return requires that we give up what had become somewhat comfortable and secure.

In our independence we judge that it would be best for us to return. We act independently to follow our own judgments. Our feelings center on the hope long felt and long unrealized that there may finally develop that "great nation" which we envisioned in our Abrahamic moment. With the return we have met another test of maturity. It shows that the period of hopelessness is over. With the reconstruction the stage is set for full personal maturity.

8

The Moment of Jesus the Christ

A. The Problem of the Historical Jesus

What do we know of the general historical background of the story of Jesus? We need to determine what we know about what is often called the "historical Jesus." The most obvious place to look would be to the gospels—Matthew, Mark, Luke and John. Before we look at these works, however, it is instructive to look at the historicity of Jesus from outside the Biblical tradition. There are Roman authors, Suetonius and Tacitus (ca. A.D. 60-120), who make reference to him, but who do not discuss him directly. "In his work on the life of Claudius, Suetonius writes (ca. A.D. 75-169) that 'since the Jews were continually making disturbances at the instigation of Chrestus, he expelled them from Rome' (Vita Claudii, xxv.5). This passage refers to the emperor Claudius' expulsion of the Jews from Rome in A.D. 49."[1] Tacitus, writing in A.D. 112-113 of the persecution of the Christians under Nero, writes also that one Christus, from whom the name of Christians is derived, was executed at the hands of the procurator Pontius Pilate in the reign of Tiberius."[2] We have here evidence for the existence of Jesus and of the place and approximate date of his crucifixion, or rather, at least of his death. This information "is probably based on the police interrogation of Christians and so is not actually independent of the New Testament or Christian tradition."[3] What these Roman authors tell us does not give us any information beyond what we can deduce from the New Testament itself. What Tacitus says in effect is that "Roman historians accepted as factual the Christian tradition that the founder of the Christian movement had been crucified by Pontius Pilate."[4]

Josephus, the Jewish historian, who wrote a detailed history of the Jews, makes only two references to Jesus in his *Antiquities*. The second of these contains the following sentences, "At this time appeared Jesus, a wise man, *if one may call him a man at all*. For he was a doer of wonderful works . . . . *This was the Christ*. And when on the denunciation of our leading men Pilate had punished him with crucifixion, those who had loved him formerly did not cease therefrom. *He appeared to them alive again* on the third day . . . ."[5] It is likely that his works are highly suspect if taken as objective fact, for they clearly have been written by a person who already believed that Jesus was the Christ. The italicized words in the passage, particularly, are probably not by Josephus. Perhaps the original text of Josephus, the Jewish writer, had been tampered with by Christian writers.

Within Jewish sources there are also references to Jesus in the Talmud. One such important reference occurs in the Babylonian Talmud. "There we find, first a Baraitha (a tradition ascribed to the first or second centuries A.D.) which reads as follows: On the eve of Passover they hanged Yeshu (of Nazareth) and the herald went before him forty days saying '(Yeshu of Nazareth) is going forth to be stoned in that he had practiced sorcery and beguiled and led astray Israel. Let everyone knowing ought in his defense come and plead for him.' But they found nought in his defense and hanged him on the eve of Passover. b Sanhedrin 43 a."[6] Interestingly, this source does give us the view that Jesus led Israel astray, that no one came to plead his case and that his death is linked with the Passover. Although such conclusions are understandable in an independent Jewish context, they add nothing to our beliefs about Jesus gained from the Gospels.

There are references to Jesus in non-Biblical Christian sources such as the Apocrypha. Within this body of material there are various gospels which "simply develop the tendency of the tradition to create legends about Jesus; others are the vehicles for teaching that came to be regarded as heretical in the church."[7] In the Gospel of Thomas, however, there are one hundred and fourteen sayings attributed to Jesus. "Its form . . . is exactly parallel to that attributed by scholars to the hypothetical synoptic gospel source Q."[8] Since the Gospel of Thomas is apparently independent of the New Testament Gospels as we have them this parallelism is interesting. Yet we have no evidence to confirm or disconfirm the actual historicity of these sayings.

Finally, in the review of the sources for the historical Jesus there are Biblical references from outside the Gospels themselves. Hayes has a helpful passage summarizing Paul's contribution to knowledge of the historical Jesus.

> From Paul . . . one would only learn that Jesus was born of a woman (Gal. 4:4), was a descendant of David (Rom. 1:3), had brothers (I Cor. 9:5) one of whom was named James (Gal. 1;19), that he broke bread and shared a cup with his followers on the night he was betrayed (I Cor. 11:23-26), was crucified, dead, buried, and on the third day was raised from the dead and appeared to various followers (I Cor. 15:4-8). In addition, Paul quotes sayings of Jesus about divorce (I Cor. 7:10-11), the meaning of the last supper (I Cor. 11:23-26), and alludes to a saying that those proclaiming the gospel should get their living by the gospel (I Cor. 9:14).[9]

Even fewer than these are references to the historical Jesus in the non-Pauline letters and in Revelation.

From this survey of the sources of the historical Jesus outside the Gospels themselves, or even outside the scriptures themselves, we may draw the following conclusion: all we know about the Jesus of general history is that he lived and died during the time of Pontius Pilate in the reign of Tiberius, Emperor of Rome.

The quest for the historical Jesus brings us, of course, to the Gospels themselves. These might seem to be accounts of the birth, life, death and resurrection of Jesus of Nazareth, who became Jesus the Christ. Of the four gospels this work accepts the view that the first three, called the synoptic gospels, have four sources. We accept the priority of Mark and the view that almost all of the Gospel was used by Matthew and Luke. Matthew and Luke had a second source of material, often called "Q," common to both of them but not employed by Mark. The authors of Matthew and Luke utilized or created materials that were unique to each of their Gospels. Thus there are four sources: Mark, Q, Matthew material and Luke material. We add the belief that the Gospel of John was written independently.

If the priority of Mark is accepted, a startling, though by no means new conclusion is forthcoming. "In 1919 Karl Ludwig Schmidt's *Der Rahmen der*

Geschichte Jesu (The Framework of the Story of Jesus) showed that the evangelist had in fact constructed his own outline.[10] Generally such a conclusion is reached on the basis of consideration of indications of the times and places of the various incidents in the life of Jesus, of particular sayings and doings attributed to him. "These investigations led to a conclusion that was to find general acceptance among critical scholars: generally speaking, the chronological and topographical narrative framework of Mark's gospel was the creation of the author . . . . If the author of Mark himself supplied the general chronological and topographical framework, then obviously the traditions which he incorporated into his Gospel, with few exceptions, came to him devoid of any framework. This conclusion shattered a long-accepted tradition that Mark had preserved in his gospel a reliable and accurate account of the life of Jesus."[11]

It follows from this conclusion that we are not in a position to write, nor do we possess, a biography of Jesus. With the acceptance of this conclusion Biblical studies moved from "source criticism" to "form criticism." They moved, that is, from a study of the sources of the Gospels to a study of the forms of stories and other units of oral tradition, which circulated prior to the writing of the Gospels themselves, prior, that is, to the writing of Mark. Examples of such units of oral tradition are miracle stories, parables or other sayings or accounts of the actions of Jesus.

With this shift in Biblical studies we get a shift of attention from the biographical framework of Jesus' life to the actual historical content of his teaching, of his particular sayings and doings. Biblical scholars needed to develop criteria for distinguishing the authentic teachings of the historical Jesus, including the reflection of teaching in specific actions he was said to perform, from those teachings of the Church about him which followed.

Norman Perrin thinks that Biblical "historical scholarship has arrived at satisfactory criteria for determining the authenticity of material attributed to the Jesus of the New Testament."[12] These criteria may be summarized as follows:

> *The criterion of dissimilarity.* . . .the fundamental criterion. Sayings and parables may be accepted as authentic if they can be shown to be dissimilar to characteristic emphases of both ancient Judaism and early Christianity . . . .

> *The criterion of multiple attestation.* . . . Briefly, themes or concerns may be accepted as authentic if they occur in different literary forms within the tradition . . . .

> *The criterion of coherence.* . . Material may be accepted as authentic if it coheres with, or is consistent with, material established as authentic by other criteria . . . .

> *The criterion of linguistic and environmental tests.* . . . Material is rejected if it is incompatible with the languages or environment of the ministry of Jesus . . . .[13]

Perrin refers to his own work, *Rediscovering the Teachings of Jesus* and to the work of R.H. Fuller in *A Critical Introduction to the New Testament*, noting the great similarity in the conclusions they each have reached independently.

Two other more recent authors have concurred in this conclusion. One is Gustaf Aulen in his *Jesus in Contemporary Historical Research*. After reviewing

"Jesus Research in the Twentieth Century," Aulen concludes that "a remarkable agreement exists, especially concerning three chief points: (1) Jesus' central message about the 'Kingdom of God' which was about to come, and his own personal relation to that event; (2) the content of Jesus' ethical proclamation; and (3) important traits in his behavior and relationship to the different streams within his own Jewish milieu."[14] I shall interpret (1), (2) and (3) to be referring to Jesus' message.

A second recent author to whom I shall refer is Michael Grant in his book *Jesus An Historian's Review of the Gospels.* Grant's thesis is reflected in the following statement: "Every thought and saying of Jesus was directed and subordinated to one single thing . . . . the realization of the Kingdom of God upon the earth."[15] This message Grant takes to be the heart of Jesus' teaching.

Grant begins his work, in the "Introduction," with an objection to the view that "no authentic life of Jesus can be written." He claims that "his public career can to a considerable extent be reconstructed."[16] Yet in reviewing certain difficulties in the Gospels he notes that "the Gospels, vague about dates and times and differing sharply, moreover, one from another, fail to provide the materials for any safe chronological framework. It is therefore not possible to offer even a likely or approximate order of events."[17] He remains consistent with this latter view when in considering miracles he argues that "it would be useless to attempt a survey of the miracles attributed to Jesus in order of time."[18]

Instead of concerning himself with the biography of Jesus' historical life, Grant, like the other authors noted above, shifts to a consideration of his teaching. "I propose to discuss, in turn, the principal themes of his mission."[19] In an Appendix on "Attitudes to the Evidence" Grant considers such criteria of acceptance as proposed by Perrin and concludes that the best way of distinguishing the authentic words and deeds of Jesus analysed by the form critics is to "look out for surprises. For anything really surprising in the Gospels is quite likely to be authentic—anything, that is to say, which clashes with what we should *expect* to find in something written after the time of Jesus."[20]

On the basis of this Biblical scholarship, what conclusions are to be drawn for the historicist perspective? The Gospels, in the main, are sacred historical writings. Each of the Gospels themselves was written well after the life, death and resurrection of Jesus. They were written by people who were Christians. They were written by people who believed that Jesus was the Christ. They were written in particular places, at particular times, for particular reasons to make particular emphases as demanded by their particular situations. On the basis of such claims as these, we may deny that the Gospels are rightly understood when they are taken to be general historical accounts of the life of the historical Jesus of Nazareth. They are, rather, proclamations of the teaching of Jesus by those who believed that Jesus Christ is Lord.

In the language of the historicist perspective they are sacred historical writings, which are based on actual general historical occurrences. We accept this conclusion of the form criticism. However, since the general historical chronological framework for these actual occurrences is not available to us, the Gospels as such contribute at best only specific bits of information to our knowledge of general history. What they do in the main is to enrich our understanding of the teachings of Jesus, of the message he was trying to convey, of the meaning of his life in the context of this message. In the language of the historicist perspective that means that they contribute to an understanding of the sacred historical moment of Jesus the Christ.

B. The Gospel of Mark

Since the priority of Mark among the written Gospel sources for the history of Jesus has been accepted in this work it seems sensible to concentrate on it in our retelling of the sacred historical story. What I will do is to follow the outline of Mark in giving what we take to be the general structure of Jesus' life, not troubling ourselves with the question as to whether this structure actually corresponds to the general history of the life of the Jesus of general history. What we are learning about is the general structure of the life of the Jesus as that was created by Mark. We are learning of him who was for Mark and is for us Jesus the Christ. In the main we are learning sacred history.

In outline, Mark's Gospel may be seen as follows: Prologue or Introduction, Mark 1:1—1:13; Jesus' Galilean ministry, Mark 1:14—9:50; Jesus' journey to Jerusalem, Mark 10:1-52; Jesus' final days in Jerusalem, Mark 11—16.

In the prologue it is noteworthy that there is no mention of Jesus' birth. References to what we call the Virgin Birth are given only in the Gospels of Matthew and Luke.

In Mark it is clear that Jesus' initial public ministry is closely associated with John the Baptist. John was seen as a fulfillment of Old Testament prophecy (See Malachi 3:1 and Isaiah 40:3). He was an ascetic figure, probably an Essene, who preached repentance and forgiveness of sin (Mark 1:4). John came before Jesus and proclaimed him mightier than he who would baptise with the Holy Spirit. John was the baptizer of Jesus, giving Godly assurance of his status.

Mark sets the stage for Jesus' public Galilean ministry with a proclamation of the kingdom of God. "The Kingdom of God is at hand" (Mark 1:15). Following Grant we may take this to be an authentic teaching of Jesus. Jesus is the prophet who proclaims the kingdom (Mark 9:1 and Mark 4:26-29). And what is the kingdom of God like? (Mark 4:30-32). It is like a grain of mustard seed. It is what all followers of Christ look forward to (Mark 9:42-48; 13:44-46). To receive the kingdom is to receive a gift as a child (Mark 10:15).

In the Galilean ministry of Jesus, Mark stresses the call to discipleship (Mark 1:16-20 and 2:13-14). There is given the list of disciples (Mark 3:16-19). (See Matthew 10:1-4; Luke 6:12-16; Acts 1:13, for other lists of disciples.) According to Mark the disciples are as follows: Simon Peter, James son of Zebedee, John son of Zebedee, Andrew, Philip, Bartholomew, Matthew, Thomas, James son of Alphaeus, Thaddaeus, Simon the Canaanean, and Judas Iscariot.

In Mark, Jesus appears to follow a non-ascetic style of life, in clear contrast to that of John (Matthew 18—20; Mark 2:15). In this connection it is stressed how Jesus clashes with Jewish leaders on matters of observance of the Law. (See Mark 2:15-17 and 7:1-8, 14-23 about eating habits. See Mark 2:18-22 about fasting. About Sabbath observances see Mark 2:23-28 and Mark 3:1-6.) Jesus thinks that the Pharisees are hypocrites in that they hold fast to the tradition of men but forsake the commandments of God (Mark 7:6-8). Jesus does not have a strict interpretation of the law (Mark 10:2-9, 17-22).

In Mark's account of Jesus' ministry there are examples of exorcising of demons (Mark 1:21-28 and 39; Mark 5:1-13; Mark 7:24-30; Mark 9:14-29). Indeed the Gospel suggests acts of exorcising as a characteristic form of Jesus' ministry. (See Mark 1:34,39). In Mark there was a woman whose daughter was possessed by an unclean spirit (Mark 7:24-30). When the woman gave evidence of a true faith Jesus says that for her faithful words the demon had left her daughter.

There are numerous instances of healing. There is the healing of Simon's mother-in-law (Mark 1:29-31); the healing of a paralytic (Mark 2:1-12); healing of a man with a withered hand, which healing was done on the Sabbath (Mark 3:1-6); the healing of the ruler of the synagogue (Mark 5:21-25), whose daughter was near death. Jesus said she was not dead but asleep. There is the healing of a blind man, requiring two touches, (Mark 8:25). Finally there is the healing of a blind beggar. It is interesting to note that there are places at which Mark editorializes about the healings. (See Mark 1:32-34; Mark 3:7-12; Mark 6:53-56).

Many of Jesus' acts can be seen as miracles, for example, the stilling of the storm (Mark 4:35-41); the feeding of the Five Thousand (Mark 6:35-44); Jesus' walking on the water (Mark 6:42-52); the feeding of the Four Thousand (Mark 8:1-10); the cursing of the fig tree (Mark 11:12-14, 20-21).

In Mark, Jesus is thought of as the Son of Man, which term occurs with considerably more frequency than the term 'Messiah.' The Son of Man has authority to forgive sins (Mark 2:10). He is Lord even of the Sabbath (Mark 2:28). The Son of Man suffers necessarily (Mark 8:31; Mark 9:9-13, 31; Mark 10:33-34; Mark 14:21-41). He will die and be resurrected. An exalted figure, the Son of Man will come in glory (Mark 8:38; 13:26: 14:62). It is noteworthy that in speaking of the Son of Man Jesus is speaking in the third person.

In the synoptics, especially in Mark, there are two passages where the phrase 'Son of Man' might mean simply 'man'. The Son of Man has authority to forgive sins (see Mark 2:10), and the Son of Man is Lord of the Sabbath. (See Mark 2:28.) "At the same time, . . . the evangelist (Mark) himself must think of 'Son of Man' as referring to one who is more than human; he is the exalted Lord who will come in glory."[21] At places Jesus is identified with the Son of Man who is in turn Son of God. (See Mark 13:32.)

When the High Priest asked Jesus whether he was the Messiah the Son of God, Jesus answered, "I am." ". . . and you will see the Son of Man sitting at the right hand of Power, and coming with the clouds of heaven" (Mark 14:62).

> Thus Mark's concept of "Son of Man" is highly developed. It is Jesus' own designation for himself and denotes one who is a man but who will also come in angelic glory; who is also Messiah and Son of God; and who will suffer and give his life for others in accordance with scriptures, and rise again. The suffering of the Son of Man is apparently connected with the figure of the righteous servant of Yahweh in Isa. 52:13—53:12. This idea that the Son of Man suffers is apparently Mark's own contribution to the doctrine, for Matthew and Luke contain it only in the passages which they derive from Mark.[22]

On the basis of this, and in summary, I think that the Son of Man suggests that Jesus the Christ is "truly man," while the view that Jesus is the Son of God suggests that he is "truly God." (See John 1:49-51.)

In Chapter ten of Mark, Jesus' journey to Jerusalem is presented. He went to fulfill his mission: "The Son of Man will be delivered into the hands of men, and they will kill him, and when he is killed, after three days he will rise'' (Mark 9:31).

Jesus shared the sentiments of the disciples that the kingdom of God was at hand. Indeed this was his initial message. Probably he went to Jerusalem to proclaim it. (Compare Luke 19:11.)

On the journey to Jerusalem he told his disciples what was going to happen to him, that he would be delivered to the chief priests, there to be condemned and delivered to the gentiles; to be mocked and spit upon, to be scourged and killed. After three days he would rise again (Mark 10:32-34).

Jesus' journey to Jerusalem was not direct. (See Mark 10:1.) The only area he did not minister in was Samaria. John's Gospel tells more of this. Jesus' ministry on the way to Jerusalem had many of the same characteristics of his Galilean ministry. There is the controversy with the Pharisees (Mark 10:2-9); the application of the Torah (Mark 10:10-12); discussions on kingship and discipleship (Mark 10:13-31); interpretation of his role on earth (Mark 10:32-35); healings (Mark 10:46-52).

Mark's account of Jesus' final days in Jerusalem begins with a depiction of his entry into the city (Mark 11:1-11). This is especially interesting for this work, for it shows the connection with David. He was seen as the new David, who was expected to establish the great nation promised to Abraham and prophesied by Isaiah. He was to fulfill the moments of the sacred history which had preceded him.

This is an outline of Jesus' week of passion, the final week of his life.

Sunday: the "triumphal entry" (Mark 11:1-11).

Monday: cleansing of the temple (Mark 11:15-19); also the cursed fig tree (Mark 11:12-14). It is a question as to why he was not arrested that day. Perhaps it is because the Jewish leadership feared him because he was popular.

Tuesday: Teaching in the temple (Mark 11:20—12:44). This material emphasizes the conflict between Jewish leaders and Jesus. In Mark Thirteen we have a collection of eschatological predictions, commonly known as the "little apocalypse" (See Mark 13:1-2). It is predicted that the temple will be destroyed.

Wednesday: At Bethany (Mark 14:1-11). The Jewish leaders were plotting to arrest Jesus and to kill him without creating a tumult. Judas consulted with the leaders about plans to betray Jesus. Jesus was annointed by a woman as if he was being prepared for burial.

Thursday: The Last Supper, agony in Gethsemane, betrayal and hearing before the High Priest and Sanhedrin (Mark 14:12-72).

Friday: Trial before Pilate, crucifixion and burial (Mark Chapter fifteen).

Saturday: Sabbath; Jesus was in the closed tomb, dead.

Sunday: Easter. Visit to the tomb by the women (Mark 16:1-8). Mary Magdalene, Mary, mother of

James and Salome are said to come to the tomb. (See Mark 15:40-41, 47.) The women discovered the stone rolled away, and they encountered a young man clothed in a white robe, who assured them that Jesus had risen. The women were supposed to go and to tell the disciples of the resurrection. (See Mark 16:9-20.) We believe this "Longer ending" is a later addition to Mark's Gospel.)

C. The Moment When He was Crucified, Dead and Buried

Jesus was crucified, and he died. We must believe that he died, really died, for if we deny this, then we cannot believe that he was fully human.

"In Gethsemane He knows that death stands before Him."[23] Mark writes that Jesus "began to be greatly distressed and troubled (Mark 14:33). He became "sorrowful" in his soul, "even to death" (Mark 14:34). "Jesus is so thoroughly human that he shares the natural fear of death. Jesus is afraid, though not as a coward. . . . He is afraid in the face of death itself. Death . . . is something dreadful."[24] We capture the full humanity of Jesus best, absolutely best, in this moment of his story. This is why it is useful to stress his sorrow and distress and trouble at this point.

Jesus already knew his mission, he knew the task which had been given him. "I have a baptism to be baptized with; and how I am constrained until it is accomplished!" (Luke 12:50). He knew his mission, yet he cried, "Father, all things are possible to thee, remove this cup from me." Jesus concluded, "Yet not what I will, but what thou wilt" (Mark 14:36). "He means only this: If this greatest of all terrors, death, must befall Me according to Thy will, then I submit to this horror."[25]

In saying "remove this cup from me," Jesus is seeking the assistance of God. He also seeks the assistance of his disciples, who show their humanity by not being able even to stay awake to be with him in his difficult hour. They are fighting off sleep in a way which seems natural and human to us all. They do not succeed, and Jesus awakens them repeatedly. Why does he want them awake? He does not want to be alone, forsaken even by his disciples. He asks Peter, 'Could you not watch one hour?' " (Mark 14:37).

The full humanity of Jesus is stressed by the author of Hebrews. "In the days of his flesh, Jesus offered up prayers and supplications, with low cries and tears, to him who was able to save him from death" (Hebrews 5:7).

We have, finally, the death scene itself. Jesus died an agonizing death. "Jesus cried with a loud voice, . . . 'My God, my God, why has thou forsaken me?' " (Mark 15:34). He has, he knows, been forsaken in Death, by the God of life. With another "loud cry" he died.

He was dead, really dead, and he was buried.

D. The Easter Moment: The Resurrection Faith

The cornerstone of the Christian faith is the belief in the resurrection of Jesus the Christ. In this sacred historical moment we are freed from all the cares and troubles of the world.

The resurrection in our sacred history is the lightest, most joyful moment of all. It is a moment of celebration that the burden of our guilt and our bondage have been taken from us. He took on the sins of the world, yet he lives. There is hope in him, even beyond the grave.

The resurrection is a moment in the sacred historical story between man and God. It was such a moment for the disciples. It is such a moment for us. It is an exodus moment, for in it we are freed from bondage. It is a Davidic moment, for in it is achieved, not by our own doing, that long awaited kingdom by which "all the families of the earth shall bless themselves."

I want to argue that the resurrection is only a moment in sacred history. This is the one moment of all our moments in which there is no general historical background. This is supported and reinforced by the fact that Jesus appeared only to his disciples, only to those who had believed, only to those who could see him or touch him with the eyes of faith, or only to those whom Jesus was specifically to bring from unbelief to belief.

Gordon Kaufman calls the resurrection the "actual historical foundation of Christian faith."[26] By this he means that "the resurrection was the event in which this belief itself was born."[27] For our purposes we may regard this to mean that the resurrection was the sacred historical moment in which those who had thought they had believed in Jesus the Christ, but who had subsequently denied him because of their misunderstandings, actually came to hold the Christian belief.

It may be shown that the resurrection was only a sacred historical event to those who believed by showing that Jesus appeared only to those who believed or to those, like Paul, whom Christ was to change from unbelief to belief. It is not to be taken as a general historical event available to all. "For I delivered you as of first importance what I also received, that Christ died for our sins in accordance with the scriptures, that he was buried, that he was raised on the third day in accordance with the scriptures, and that he appeared to Cephas, then to the twelve. Then he appeared to more than five hundred brethren at one time, most of whom are still alive, though some have fallen asleep. Then he appeared to James, then to all the apostles. Last of all, as to one untimely born, he appeared also to me" (I Corinthians 15:3-8).

The appearances of the resurrected Christ have a strange character befitting the idea we have of the spiritual or resurrection body. "For example, the sudden and inexplicable appearance and disappearance of the resurrected Jesus (e.g., Luke 24:31, 36), his apparent going through locked doors at will (e.g., John 20:19, 26), and the fact that the disciples doubted they were really seeing the dead Jesus alive again (note here not only Thomas' well-known doubt (John 20:24-27), but also reports in Matthew (28:17) and Luke 24:21-31, 41) all suggest the non-physical character of the appearances"[28] What we can infer from the strangeness or non-physical character of these appearances is that they were not empirical general historical events potentially witnessable by any person of any persuasion. The non-physical appearances were experiences in the sacred history of the disciples and others.

In the resurrection moment we know that we are saved from ourselves, from all the temptations of the woman in the garden in the beginning, of Noah, of Abraham, of David, of all the Biblical characters. In this moment we know that our freedom from bondage to ourselves is given to us. It cannot be something we gain by our own efforts. So we surrender ourselves to God in Christ, who saves us, who sets us free from ourselves, who gives us a new beginning. And he calls us to go forth "and make disciples of all nations, baptizing them in the name of the Father and of the Son and of the Holy Spirit, teaching them to observe all that" he has commanded of us. And he is with us always "to the close of the age," that is, to the end of time (Matthew 28:19-20).

And, like Isaiah, we say, "Here am I, send me" (Isaiah 6:8). God in Christ is with us, and by us ". . . all the families of the earth shall bless themselves." It is at this season of the spirit, when we have the resurrection faith in our lives, that we truly know what it is to let God in Christ be Lord of our histories.

At the moment of the resurrection when the disciples had come together with Jesus "they asked him, 'Lord, will you at this time restore the kingdom to Israel?' He said to them, 'It is not for you to know times or seasons. . . . But you shall receive power when the Holy Spirit has come upon you; and you shall be my witnesses in Jerusalem and . . . to the end of the earth.' And when he had said this, as they were looking on, he was lifted up, and a cloud took him out of their sight" (Acts 1:6-9).

E. In Him all Previous Moments are Relived and Fulfilled

The moment of Jesus the Christ, the moment of his birth, life, death, and resurrection, is the moment in the sacred historical story when all previous moments are relived and fulfilled. By this claim I mean to say three things. First, he can and is to be understood as reliving the various moments, e.g. he is the new Abraham who met his test, willing to sacrifice everything just to be faithful. He is the new Moses who leads us out of bondage into freedom.

Secondly, however in him all the previous moments are fulfilled. In him the Abrahamic moment is fulfilled, for he is the Lamb that God himself said he would provide. In answer to a question from Isaac, Abraham prophesied that God would provide a lamb, and that was not at the time to be Isaac. In him the Moses moment is fulfilled. Moses under God led the people from bondage to freedom. And in him we find the freedom into which we are led.

Thirdly, to say that in him all previous moments are relived and fulfilled is to say something about ourselves, for whom God in Christ is Lord. It is to say that in him we relive the moments, the times of Abrahamic trial, the times of Mosaic freedom. If we are in Christ we again know all the seasons of the spirit through which we have passed, and we know the fulfillment found in him.

A qualification must be made immediately. There is one moment for which this is not true. That is the moment of the Fall. At the season of the Fall I said that there was created the problem for which the rest of the Biblical story is the answer. Christ is that answer given to us in its fullest form. Christ is not in the Fall, although Christ is before the Fall and after the Fall, in all the other moments. But the signs or marks of the moment of the Fall were temptation and the succumbing to it. Insofar as Christ is fully human, we are not able to say that he was entirely free of temptation. To this extent, then, the moment of the Fall was in him. But we cannot say that the succumbing to temptation was in him. Nor can we say that when we succumb to temptation we are in him. Christ is in the moment of the Fall only partially.

There are in him the beginning moments, first the moment of creation. Just as creation in the beginning was "out of nothing," so there is in him a new creation out of nothing. There is the new creation of the resurrected body of Christ out of nothingness following the death of Jesus. He lived in this new moment, and, since he, in being the first born of the dead, atoned for us all, his new birth fulfills all that had happened in the past sacred history.

In him we relive the new creation as did the disciples of old. The hopes and expectations of all who beheld him were dashed. Even Peter denied him three times. Out of this psychological and spiritual nothingness came the resurrected Christ. Out of the dashed hopes came faith in them, just as it comes in us. In him we are a new creation. The past is finished and gone. Everything in us is fresh and new. We are forgiven. Out of those who believed and out of us who now believe comes the Church.

In him there is recovered what we had in the garden before the Fall, unbroken communion with God, who again in Christ becomes Lord of our histories. In him and in his relation to others there was recreated the unbroken communion with God and fellow man which was in the beginning in the garden. He is the fulfillment of the garden, for in him we have the unbroken communion with God and with others. In him we need not be naked and ashamed before each other. In him we are joined in the bond of Christian fellowship.

In him is the world washed clean, as it was by the flood at the time of Noah. Just as Noah lived during the flood which cleanses the world, so Jesus the Christ lived during the coming of the kingdom of God, which cleanses the world. The kingdom, inaugurated by Jesus the Christ, is the fulfillment of the earlier cleansing attempt. For us to enter into this kingdom is for us to be cleansed.

He was the new Abraham who was sorely tried but who met his test, who was faithful to the end, and who demonstrated in his life and death what it means to let God be the Lord of his life. At the time of his greatest test he said, "Not what I will, but what thou wilt." In him are the promises of God to Abraham fulfilled, for his kingdom is the great nation which God had promised to Abraham and by whom all the families of the earth shall bless themselves." In him we relive the moments of Abrahamic trial and steadfastness of faith, and so do we take God in Christ as Lord.

He is the new Moses whom God calls to lead us from bondage into freedom. In him there is an exodus from slavery to our sins, an exodus out of the domination of Rome, an exodus into the kingdom of God. In him is the Moses moment fulfilled. Moses led the people to the Promised Land. Jesus the Christ in his kingdom is the Promised Land, to which we are led. In him we know freedom from bondage. Through Moses God gave bread to the people in the wilderness. This bread sustained the people in their lives. In him we take a step beyond Moses, for he is the bread of life.

With him we celebrate a new passover in which we are washed in the blood of the lamb as were those of old who took the passover meal before the original exodus. In the new passover there is a reliving of the experience of being brought out of bondage into freedom. In the Lord's Supper there is the real presence of Christ, and the real experience of being brought out of bondage into freedom. In the Lord's Supper there is the real presence of Christ, and the real experience of being delivered from all that binds us.

Jesus the Christ relived the time in the wilderness both during the days he was in temptation and during the years he was in the world and the world knew him not. In this wilderness he gave us the law of love in his sayings and doings and in his commandment that we should love our neighbors as ourselves. He is the fulfillment of the wilderness and the Law given to us for in him we have a new covenant with the Lord God. He will be our God and we will be his people if we live in him.

In him is the new wilderness into which we are led when we know not what our new life in Christ will be. In him we are identified as the people who live by this law. He has shown us the way.

He relived the moment of the conquest and settlement. Just as the people of God of old crossed the Jordan into a foreign world so He came into our world which knew him not. Just as the people entered and conquered the land so God in Christ enters the world and conquers it. In the inauguration of his kingdom he fulfills the inauguration of the kingdom of Israel in Saul and then in David.

In him we come to the place, that spiritual state, which God has chosen for us, just as the people of old found, conquered and settled in the Promised Land, the land that God showed to them. Biblical Christianity is not tied to a physical land. God in Christ and his kingdom is that land to which God brings us.

In him there was relived the moment of David, for he was the new David, the perfect holy man and the perfect kingly ruler combined. The problems of divided loyalties between God and king are resolved in him just as they were in David. Yet in him also was the moment of David fulfilled, for in him was the inauguration of the kingdom of which David's kingdom was but a foreshadowing.

In him as in David we find in ourselves a unity both with the people of God and with each other. In him we find the long-awaited, long-hoped-for kingdom by which "all the families of the earth shall bless themselves."

We see him in the prophecies of Isaiah. He is the "shoot from the stump of Jesse" on whom the spirit of God rests, "and the government will be upon his shoulder, and his name will be called 'Wonderful, Counselor, Mighty God, Everlasting Father, Prince of Peace' " (Isaiah 9:6). He fulfilled these prophecies, first in the recognition of the crowd on "Palm Sunday" that he came as a Davidic ruler, and secondly with the inauguration of his kingdom. In him we live in the hope like that proclaimed by Isaiah and in the quietness and trust which is our strength.

In him was the hopelessness which attended the fall of Jerusalem. He relived the loss of hope when he gave his will to God in the garden of Gethsemane and later was crucified. At this point there no longer seemed any hope just as there no longer seemed any hope that the Messiah would come after the city of David was destroyed. In him is the fulfillment of this time of hopelessness, for it was to be through him, in spite of the death of Jesus, that the hope was actually to come. In him we relive moments of hopelessness when, like Peter, we deny him, when we find ourselves caught in the stuff of which we were made.

In the exile the hopelessness of the fall of Jerusalem moment was compounded. Not only was Jerusalem destroyed but the people had been removed from Jerusalem, and the conditions under which there could be a rekindling of hope seemed remote. This exile state was in him following the crucifixion. The disciples had been completely separated from him. He was gone. To them there seemed no way that hope in him could possibly be recovered. In him, however, this compounded hopelessness is fulfilled, for he is given to us as the resurrected Christ in a way beyond our control or understanding.

And in the exile moment there is in us the belief that our warfare is ended and our iniquity is pardoned. And in this belief we are comforted. In him every valley will be lifted up. "He was wounded for our transgressions . . . , with his stripes we are healed" (Isaiah 53:5). "And the glory of the Lord shall be revealed" (Isaiah 40:15).

The hope for his coming was rekindled in the return of the people and the rebuilding of the city and the temple. He was in that return and reconstruction, and that was fulfilled in his resurrection. Instead of a reconstruction there is for him the building of the kingdom of God. In his resurrection and in his inauguration of the kingdom we know the release of all our burdens and the fulfillment of all our hopes.

In him all the moments of the sacred historical story are relived and fulfilled.

F. The Maturity of Jesus the Christ

I will say that in the life of Jesus the Christ we see the fully mature person. We see him in whom the quest for maturity has ended. We see an adult person in the commendable states of both independence and self-sufficiency on the one hand and dependence and self-insufficiency on the other hand. There is a dynamic between these poles of maturity in his life. When circumstances require it or when he judges it is for the best he will move in a dynamic pattern from pole to pole, even from a self-sufficiency to self-insufficiency. In reflecting all these states of maturity in his life he completes the moments of maturity we have considered from the beginning moments to the moments of return and reconstruction. He completes all of them, for in him we see the full range of the dynamic movement between the poles of maturity.

As a mature person we see Jesus being able to step out of any situation alone and independently, making practically wise judgments for himself. We see one who is able to display a steadiness of his feeling states especially as reflected in his behavior. We see one who is socially mature, who lives within the social structures of his day, but who steps out of this at significant times in his life. In his stepping out of his cultural and religious milieu he becomes the founder of Christianity.

In his life he observed the requirements and met the restrictions imposed upon him in his role in the community in which he found himself, including his family. Unlike the natural man in the beginning he was not completely immersed in this web of dependencies. Nor was he entirely dependent upon it. Yet he freely entered into it. In this there was a measure of independence.

Like Noah he had a vision of the society and the state of mankind as a whole. In this, as was in the case of Noah, he knew the maturity of self-sufficiency. When he proclaimed that "the kingdom of God is at hand" he, like the mature Noah, envisioned a whole new state for mankind. In his "Sermon on the Mount" he did look at the inner man making judgments about the evil in the imagination of man.

There is much of the great maturity of Abraham in Jesus the Christ. I believe that we see the closest analogue between Abrahamic maturity and the maturity of Jesus. In Abrahamic maturity there is a vision of a "great nation," and there is the independent judgment enough to sustain that vision. This is fulfilled in Jesus' vision of "the kingdom of God."

There is the Abrahamic independence, yet not the lack of self-sufficiency. The mature Jesus gained an independent sense of his mission; he exhibited the steadiness of judgment and behavior to carry that through. In this sort of self-sufficiency he completes the maturity of Abraham. That completion is found in his inauguration of what he called "the kingdom of God." This was Abraham's "great nation" fulfilled.

Like Abraham he was able to do that because of his self-sufficiency, his ability to go on in spite of great obstacles. In his Garden of Gethsemane moment he displayed the Abrahamic ability to remain steadfast even in his lack of understanding. Like Abraham in his maturity he was able to show steadiness because he was dependent even self-sufficient before that which called him to his mission. Time and time again he displayed that Abrahamic resignation. In this was his self-insufficiency.

In his maturity Jesus the Christ knows the bondage of people, even that radical Egypt sort of bondage which renders them self-insufficient. He was able to step out of his bondage and know the exodus liberating freedom from such bondage. In this was his independence. In this were the conditions necessary for being free to enter into the web of dependencies in his society. In his freedom and independence he acted to create the conditions for a new people. Such creation can be traced back to his "Last Supper" held with his disciples on the occasion of the Jewish passover. That itself was an exodus in which this mature person led a people from bondage to freedom. It was a point of passage into the "great nation" initially envisioned by an independent Abraham and converted by Jesus into "the kingdom of God."

In the life of Jesus as that is given in the rehearsal of the sacred historical story there is nothing of the meaningless freedom of the first moment of the wilderness. In his maturity Jesus is able to step out from his natural web of dependencies and even the religious law which bound him and his people. In his independence he himself devised a new law, a new covenant, wherein others could find a new identification and reorientation. In this he displayed the maturity of self-sufficiency. On nothing but his own practical judgment for the best for mankind he set forth his Great Commandment. In this he willingly bound himself being the clearest reflection of his own teaching. In this he found a new meaning and purpose. In this he offered a new orientation for himself and for others, an orientation which provides a new basis for emotional and social stability.

In his maturity he knew nothing of the second moment in the wilderness. There was in him such a steadiness of behavior in accordance with what he judged to be practically best for him that he did not know the negative freedom of falling short in faithfulness to his own law. He was mature enough to be dependent on the law of love.

In his maturity Jesus the Christ himself knew nothing of the ups and downs following the conquest and settlements of developing maturity. He had the intellectual capacity to devise his message and to remain true to his mission when he came to understand it. He moved independently as he stepped out of his social and religious milieu to preach and teach. He did not win over the people whom he addressed quickly or impressively. Indeed in his mature and wise judgment he saw what that would have meant, and he made his presentation of his message intentionally hard to perceive.

In his steadiness he knew no ups and downs. He was beyond the adolescent stage as reflected in the Deuteronomic success formula. In his maturity he had the steadiness to be his own permanent Davidic ruler. In his independence he exercised his own judgment. In his steadiness and faithfulness to his Lord he showed a mature dependence, even at times a self-sufficiency. In him was ushered in a period of success and unity, a Davidic state elevated only after his death into the inauguration of the kingdom of God.

Unlike David he did not act un-kingly, and in him was no fall from the success and unity. Yet in him was the quietness and trust and confidence of the Isaiah moment of maturity. He even showed the independence of mind and the dependence of his God to wait even in the most difficult of circumstances prior to his crucifixion. He knew the difficulty of waiting and of being patient when there was no clear sense of what he could do for himself. His intellectual and emotional steadiness reflected itself in his behavior. In him was the rock on which he could stand firmly even in his darkest hour.

In his maturity Jesus the Christ knows moments of self-insufficiency to his Lord. This is not, however, the sort of self-insufficiency known in the hopelessness of the exile moment. He was not completely subject to forces beyond his control.

He was dependent, however, on the constancies of life as he lived it with his web of dependencies. He did not need to rely on these because he had an independence and a personal steadiness of his own. From deep within himself came forth a rock firm enough to provide him clarity of vision and purpose. He provided out of his independent practical judgment the rules which defined his own life.

Finally he remained steady and clearly aware of the "great nation" which he himself would inaugurate. In his steadiness in his vision of this he showed both independence of mind and a dependence on his Lord, who would usher in this kingdom.

9

Growing in the Maturity of Christ

After the moment of Jesus the Christ, after the resurrection, there is a new beginning. The sacred historical story has come to an end. The dynamic movement of the sacred historical story from the beginning to the moment of Jesus the Christ has reached its culmination. The development and dynamics of maturity have been fulfilled in him.

In him there is the opportunity of a new beginning, an opportunity for growing in the maturity of Jesus the Christ. This new beginning is found in the moment when the Christian Church was born. This is the moment at the day of Pentecost when the disciples were all together, "And suddenly a sound came from heaven like the rush of a mighty wind. . . . And they were all filled with the Holy Spirit" (Acts 2:2-4).

Those who watched and heard the strange speaking in other tongues wondered whether these Galileans were not "filled with new wine" (Acts 2:13). Peter stood to address those present, and told how this outpouring of the Spirit was prophesied by Joel: "And in the last days it shall be, God declares, that I will pour out my Spirit upon all flesh, and your sons and your daughters shall prophesy, and your young men shall see visions, and your old men shall dream dreams" (Acts 2:17). And there will be all manner of wonders in the heavens above and wonders on the earth (Acts 2:19 adapted).

Peter then proclaimed that it was in God's plan that Jesus would be crucified by men and resurrected by God (Acts 2:23-24). "Being therefore exalted at the right hand of God, and having received from the Father the promise of the Holy Spirit, he has poured out this which you see and hear" (Acts 2:33). The answer for human kind: "Repent and be baptized everyone of you in the name of Jesus Christ for the forgiveness of your sins; and you shall receive the gift of the Holy Spirit" (Acts 2:38).

In this day of Pentecost, this moment when the Church was born, is a moment when we are given the gift or gifts of the Holy Spirit. From God in Christ we have been given a gift, a "comforter," a presence, which is with us in the world, in our sacred historical experience. This spirit given to us in this moment of our lives will be that which will enable us to grow.

The Spirit, though, is not new. It is a reality in our sacred historical relation with God, the presence of God in the resurrected Christ who is with us and who counsels us. When God in Christ is our Lord we are prepared to receive the gifts of the Spirit. We are taken possession of, and in spite of ourselves, we are given power. What is new in Pentecost is a fellowship created by the Spirit, and this fellowship we call the Church. This fellowship is a new creation, a creation of the Spirit, who, on the day of Pentecost, "came from heaven like the rush of a mighty wind." The fellowship provides a context for our growth in maturity.

To say that the Church is of the Holy Spirit is not to be taken to mean that there is no connection between the Church and the work of Christ. As Gustaf Aulen puts it, "The finished work of Christ is the foundation of the church; . . . and . . . the church appears as his continuing work . . . . Christ has become embodied in the church . . . . The church is, therefore, a creation through the act of God in Christ. This may also be expressed in this way: the church is the fellowship created by the Holy Spirit."[1]

In our discussion of the historical Jesus we concluded that we cannot be sure of the chronological and topographical framework of his life and work. We simply do not know, as a matter of general historical fact, whether or not Jesus founded a church. It does seem clear, however, that the Gospel writers did not believe that Jesus founded a Church. This is the conclusion of Hans Kung in his work *The Church* when he writes that "in the pre-Easter period, during his lifetime Jesus did not found a Church."[2] In the Gospel accounts Jesus "never addressed himself merely to a select group separated from the mass of people."[3] His relation with the twelve disciples, which is depicted as special, "illustrates precisely not the singling out of the select few, but the calling of Israel as a whole."[4]

Kung argues that "in the *pre-Easter period*, Jesus, by his preaching and ministry, *laid the foundations* for the emergence of a post-resurrection Church."[5] The Church existed, says Kung, "*from the time of faith in the resurrection.* As soon as men gathered together in faith in the resurrection of the crucified Jesus of Nazareth and in expectation of the coming consummation of the reign of God and the return of the risen Christ in glory, the Church came into existence."[6]

We need a time to locate all these phenomena in the minds and hearts of individual men. We need also a time when there came into being a fellowship of such like-minded people. That time, I claim, was Pentecost. Thus it is that the Church stands as a creation by God in Christ at Pentecost.

What was created was a fellowship bound together by the Holy Spirit, who poured upon men that day the gifts of the Holy Spirit. What are these gifts? Here we turn appropriately to Paul, to Corinthians.

> Now there are varieties of gifts, but the same Spirit; and there are varieties of service, but the same Lord; and there are varieties of working, but it is the same God who inspires them all, in every one. To each is given the manifestation of the Spirit for the common good. To one is given through the Spirit the utterance of wisdom, and to another the utterance of knowledge according to the same Spirit, to another faith by the same Spirit; to another gifts of healing by the one Spirit, to another the working of miracles, to another prophecy, to another the ability to distinguish between spirits, to another various kinds of tongues, to another the interpretation of tongues. All these are inspired by one and the same Spirit, who apportions to each one individually as he wills (First Corinthians 12:4-11).

All those with such diverse gifts are organically related together in one body with Christ as the head.

Life in the Church becomes a beginning point and a context for the growth of maturity in Jesus Christ. To grow in the Church is to develop the gift or gifts of the Spirit we have been given, and to let others develop their own variety of these gifts. We grow in openness to others in the fellowship. We know that independence of which maturity is made as we have our own relationship to God, and as we nurture that gift which we have been given. We know also our dependence on the fellowship itself and on the expressed gifts of others.

We grow in the maturity of Christ in our lives in the Church in that we see a foreshadowing of that kingdom which was inaugurated in him. In the Church is that great nation promised to Abraham. In entering the Church we again enter the Promised Land. In taking the Lord's Supper we again know the freedom from bondage we knew in our exodus moment of spiritual maturity. The Church is that great Davidic nation with Christ, who came as the image of David, as our head. The new David in Christ is the spiritual head, and the Church is that body that foreshadows the establishment of God's spiritual kingdom to be, and which also looks back to the garden moment which was in the beginning.

We see more about growth in the maturity of Christ in the life and message of St. Paul. Saul, an educated and cosmopolitan person, independently and effectively was persecuting the Christians. Then as he was traveling one day on the road to Damascus he had an experience which turned him around. The resurrected Christ appeared to him. In him the historical Jesus became a spiritual reality, a saviour God.

Groping in blindness after his exodus from bondage Saul, now become Paul, displayed intellectual maturity and emotional steadiness. He retired into Arabia, perhaps to the "Rose City" of Petra, for reflection on what had happened to him and on what it all meant. He returned, after having decided in his maturity, to be a witness of Christ to the Gentiles. In his three missionary journeys and on his final trip to Rome, he was even more mature in his effectiveness in witnessing for Christ than he had been in his persecutions of Christians.

We get a clear view of the message of Paul in his letter to the Romans, especially Chapters one through eight. Paul begins his letter with a general introduction in Romans 1:1-15, in which he gives the classic Christian greeting: "Grace to you and peace from God our Father and the Lord Jesus Christ" (Romans 1:7b). Following this introductory section he gives the theme of the whole letter. He, Paul, is not "ashamed of the Gospel: it is the power of God for salvation to every one who has faith . . . . For in it the righteousness of God is revealed through faith for faith" (Romans 1:16,17). Here Paul is stating an essential feature of the mature man in Christ, an ability to stand on one's own, as for example, Noah did in building the Ark, or as Abraham did in traveling to Moriah. Here is the maturity of self-sufficiency.

This position of Paul's stands out clearly in Romans 1:18—3:20, in which section Paul describes life without the Gospel, life not lived under the Lordship of God in Christ. Paul tells us directly that by our wickedness, by the succumbing to temptations which caused the woman in the garden to fall, we "suppress the truth" (Romans 1:18). "Ever since the creation of the world his (God's) invisible nature . . . has been clearly perceived in the things that have been made" (Romans 1:20). So we are without excuse who do not let God in Christ be Lord of our lives. We are immature in that we have neither an emotional steadiness or a practically wise judgment.

Moreover, we cannot save ourselves by our own efforts, or in the Pauline Biblical way of speaking, by doing good works. Over and over again we have seen the heroes of faith fall away from their calling by God. We have seen God take everything away from us, except our faith, to test that faith, for example in Abraham. We have had to develop the maturity of independence, even self-sufficiency. We have seen God dash our expectations for the coming of the Kingdom, as in the case of Peter and the disciples, so that men might be prepared to receive Jesus Christ as Lord.

Paul is well aware of all this and he minces no words: "For no human being will be justified in his sight by works of the law" (Romans 3:20). Paul's reason is simple, yet sufficient: All that we get through doing good works, or trying to follow the law, or trying to save ourselves, is knowledge of our own sin (Romans 3:20). All we get when, like the woman in the garden, we elevate ourselves to the rank of little gods, is knowledge that we are unable to save ourselves.

For the Biblical Christian there is a growth into this Pauline stage. In one sense there is going on in Paul the dynamics of bondage and freedom which we encountered in the exodus and wilderness and law moments. Paul was bound to the law in his days of persecution. He was freed from that law on the road to Damascus. Having been so freed he is rebound to Christ who turned him around. The former law, then, has no hold on him, at least in the sense that it does not provide a positive constructive model for his actions. It did, however, have the function of reminding him of his sin. On the basis of the law he was able to judge that he had not faithfully followed it.

He, or any person in his Pauline moment, has the maturity to realize the function of the law in the development of the spirit. The people in the second moment in the wilderness did not make such a judgment; they were themselves judged. Paul in his maturity makes the practically wise judgment of his own shortcomings under the law, and he displays the emotional steadiness to witness consistently under his bondage to the Lordship of Christ. The Pauline person has grown in the maturity of Christ.

In Romans 3:21—4:25 Paul shows us what it is for God in Christ to be our Lord. Paul's question here is this: what is the Gospel of Jesus Christ for man? His answer: man is saved by faith, that by God's grace, which is a gift, we may receive Christ into our lives as our Lord, our one and only authority in matters of faith and action. In his own words "since all have sinned and fallen short of the glory of God, they are justified by his grace as a gift, through the redemption which is in Christ Jesus" (Romans 3:23-24).

Suitably, Paul refers at this point to Abraham who "believed God, and it was reckoned to him as righteousness" (Romans 4:3). Abraham was saved by his faith, not by what he did, not by his good works. Abraham was saved because even when all was taken from him, even when he was ready to sacrifice everything in order that he might be faithful, even in all this God was still the Lord of his life. In Abraham was the independence to go to Moriah, yet the dependence on God who called him to go.

In Romans 5:1—8:39 Paul tells us what life under the Gospel is like, what it is for God in Christ to be Lord. God has shown us this life "in that while we were yet sinners Christ died for us" (Romans 5:8). God brought us into his world giving us everything we needed. We were to acknowledge him as Lord. Instead, in the freedom he also gave us, we have sinned, for we have chosen to be unfaithful, to choose ourselves to serve rather than the Lord God. Sin came into the world through one woman and death through sin. And sin and the wages of sin "spread to all men because all men sinned" (Romans 5:12). And we have seen this record of the falling short in faithfulness over and over again in our sacred rehearsal from the woman in the garden, from Noah, Abraham, Moses, David and from each of our sacred historical moments.

Paul, a former Jew, wrestles with the concept of law, which, ironically has the function of increasing our knowledge of sin: "Sin indeed was in the world before the law was given, but sin is not counted where there is no law" (Romans 5:13). In a sense there is no sin where there is no law. At the least we become aware of our sinful condition, of our acts of negative freedom in response to what God has called us to do and be. Interestingly, the commentary of the Oxford Annotated Bible suggests that it was God's purpose to make us aware of our sinful condition in giving us the law.[7]

In his progressive self-revelation God in Christ gives us the law at a time in our spiritual development when we need it. After being freed from bondage and being in the condition of not being tied down by and identified with anything, we need the regulation of the law. We need specific guidance.

In Christ in whom all the sacred historical moments are fulfilled and in whom we see God as fully as we are allowed to see him, the law is dispensable. In Paul's words: "You have died to the law through the body of Christ, so that you may belong to another, to him who has been raised from the dead in order that we may bear fruit for God" (Romans 7:4). We are, in other words, "discharged from the law, dead to that which held us captive" (Romans 7:6).

Now we no longer are to take a set of legal and therefore good works as a model for what it is to be faithful. The law no longer gives us a positive constructive model for what it is to be faithful. The law may continue to provide a model negatively. We may say, for example, that the law is a guide, a guide as to what we may not do. Even this, however, is not to be taken at face value, for under certain circumstances, bearing false witness, for example, we may have to set aside the law just to be faithful. Setting aside the law under unusually difficult circumstances is precisely what Abraham did.

We are given a positive and constructive model in Jesus the Christ who shows us fully what it is for God in Christ to be Lord. Not only does he show us, providing us an example. He also gives himself for us, dying for us, and thereby conquering the death to which our shortcomings are inevitably to lead us. We are saved by the faith that, in Christ this has happened. We are saved by acknowledging God in Christ as Lord.

The kingdom of which Mark so forcefully wrote has been inaugurated but not established. We await it in eager expectation. We long for it. "For the creation waits with eager longing for the revealing of the sons of God, . . . because the creation itself will be set free from its bondage to decay and obtain the glorious liberty of the children of God" (Romans 8:19,21).

Meanwhile, "we know that in everything God works for good with those who love him, who are called according to his purpose" (Romans 8:28). We ask, "If God is for us who can be against us?" (Romans 8:31). We acknowledge God as Lord and we know that we cannot be separated from our Lord by tribulation, or distress, or persecution, or famine, or nakedness, or peril, or sword (Romans 8:35). For, says Paul, "I am sure that neither death nor life, nor angels, nor principalities, nor things present, nor things to come, nor powers, nor height, nor depth, nor anything else in all creation, will be able to separate us from the love of God in Christ Jesus our Lord" (Romans 8:38-39).

As with David, it is ironic that the man who says and confesses these things, the man Paul, for whom we are sure that Christ is Lord of his history, that this man also says, "For I do not do what I want, but I do the very thing I hate" (Romans 7:15). Or he says, "Wretched man that I am! Who will deliver me from this body of death?" (Romans 7:24).

The lesson is plain: to have God in Christ as Lord and to be fully mature we have to renounce all claims for ourselves to be "like God, knowing good and evil" for our own lives. To let God in Christ be Lord is to surrender ourselves to him, so that there is one and only one absolute authority for what we are, what we feel and what we think and do. Only in such a way can we say as Christ our Lord said, "Not what I will, but what thou wilt."

For the earliest Christians like Paul, and, perhaps, for us now also, there is the adjustment we must make who await the establishment of the Kingdom of Christ which was inaugurated in him. The faithful Christian will grow in the fellowship of the Church and the Pauline dependence on the savior God who also turns us around in our moments when he appears to us.

Yet there is a new context for growth in this moment of adjustment. It is a fivefold moment: remembrance, expectation, waiting, working and hoping. In remembering we look back to the sacred historical moments we have rehearsed, and we appreciate the various aspects of the mature Christian life seen in Jesus the Christ in whom all these moments are relived and fulfilled. In remembering we pick out times of independence, as for example in Abraham, or self-sufficiency as in the Noah or Davidic moments in our development. We remember times of dependence as in the moment of bondage to the law or even the radical self-sufficiency of the fall of Jerusalem or exile moments.

Our remembering feeds our sense of expectation, for what we specifically remember we can project into the future. Here we are reminded of the prophecies of Isaiah. As his words gave comfort or strength to the people in exile, so our expectations fanned by our remembrances help us to grow in the maturity of Christ. In him in whom all these remembered moments are relived and fulfilled our expectations comfort us, giving us the opportunity to exercise our practically wise judgments, our emotional steadiness and our social maturity. Our remembrances and our expectations are shared by us and others in the fellowship in the Church.

Since we are in an interim time we wait, and we must wait in patience. In the maturity of Christ we have grown. Our waiting is not like that Isaiah called upon us to do in the days surrounding our fall of Jerusalem moments. In our developed maturity we wait in our sense of expectation fixed as it is by our remembrances.

This time of waiting is not apathetic, nor is it hopeless. During this time we grow by working in our own ways, small or large and important, towards the end which we expect will come. In this working we will need to exercise our independent judgments as to what is the best way to proceed. We will have to have that emotional steadiness that is part of patience. Insofar as we are working in the context of the Church we will exercise our dependency on the judgment of others. Most of all, however, we will work under our dependency to Christ who showed us the way in his own work.

We also hope, and our hope is strengthened by our remembrances, our expectations and our work. On the other hand our hope enlivens the expectations and the work. It is this hope which so much helps us to grow in maturity in Christ.

We are the people who have a special hope. We are the people with a vital sense of longing for what is to come, a sense that what we remember, what we expect, what we are patiently waiting for is a reality that will come. In our hope is a vital anticipation.

Our problem is not the same as those in the earliest Church. Our problem is how to deal with the fact that the kingdom has not dawned, that the new age has not yet come, even after almost two thousand years. Many in the early Church were quite clear that the kingdom was coming soon. They did not need to ask the question "when?" What should our belief be on this question?

There would, speaking logically, seem to be three alternatives. First, we may believe, as did many in the early Church, that the end is still near at hand. We can continue with the same belief. This point of view is, I think, an important one, perhaps the dominant one, in the New Testament. Jesus had proclaimed that the kingdom of God was at hand. This emphasis, as we have seen, was one of the characteristics of Mark's gospel as stated in its theme in 1:15: "The Kingdom of God is at hand." We may understand "at hand" here to mean imminent. In Mark the imminence of the coming of the kingdom is again sugested: "Truly, I say to you, there are some standing here who will not taste death before they see the kingdom of God come with power" (Mark 9:1). Matthew agrees: some standing here who will not taste death before they see the Son of man coming in his Kingdom" (Matthew 16:28). An example from Luke may be found in the parable of the pounds (Luke 19:11-27), which he told "because they supposed that the kingdom of God was to appear immediately" (Luke 19:11). Other parables clearly stress the necd for preparedness in the face of an impending crisis; such are the servants of the absent householder (Mark 13:33-37; cf. Luke 12:35-38), the faithful and unfaithful servants (Matt. 24:45-51; Luke 12:42-46), and the thief at night (Matt. 24:43-44; Luke 12:39-40).[8]

This theme of the thief in the night is picked up at many places in the New Testament. Matthew in commenting on the coming of the thief says: "Therefore you also must be ready; for the Son of man is coming at an hour you do not expect" (Matthew 24:44). Paul comments that we need have nothing written to us concerning the times and seasons that the Lord will "descend from heaven." He says: "For you yourselves know well that the day of the Lord will come like a thief in the night" (I Thessalonians 5:2). (See also Revelation 3:3; 16:15 and 2 Peter 3:10.)

That the kingdom is at hand is clear and explicit in the Revelation to John. At the beginning of the book, in 1:3, it says, "For the time is near," and at the book's end the same theme is expressed twice: "Do not seal up the words of the prophecy of this book, for the time is near" and "Behold, I am coming soon" (Revelation 22:10 and 12). "He who testifies to these things says, 'Surely I am coming soon.' Amen. Come, Lord Jesus!" (Revelation 22:20).

When the disciples had come together they asked the risen Lord whether at this time he would restore the kingdom to Israel. "He said to them, 'It is not for you to know times or seasons which the Father has fixed by his own authority. But you shall receive power when the Holy Spirit has come upon you' " (Acts 1:7-8a). One implication here is that again the kingdom of God is at hand. For our part we are to get ready. When it comes is for God to decide.

A second response to the delay in the coming of the kingdom in the end may be the opposite—that we give up our faith that the kingdom will come. Since it

hasn't come, even yet, John, to whom the revelations came in the last book of the
Bible, is simply wrong. It just is not coming.

But this second response which denies that the kingdom will come may take
another form, that of interpreting our hope as a present possession, as something
that has already come. This too, like the first alternative, is an important emphasis in the New Testament. In a recent book Michael Grant stresses the importance of this point of view: "Every thought and saying of Jesus was directed and
subordinated to one single thing . . . : the realization of the Kingdom of God
upon the earth."[9] As one piece of scriptural support for his claim Grant quotes
Luke who recounts the incident when Jesus came to Nazareth and entered the
Synagogue on the Sabbath day as was his custom.[10] He read the scroll from Isaiah
61:1, that "the Spirit of the Lord is upon me, because the Lord has anointed
me to preach good news to the poor. He has sent me to proclaim release to the
captives and recovering of sight to the blind, to set at liberty those who are oppressed, to proclaim the acceptable year of the Lord" (Luke 4:18-19). After clos-
ing the book, Luke reports, Jesus said, "Today this scripture has been fulfilled in
your hearing" (Luke 4:21).

In Luke 11:20 we read: "If it is by the finger of God that I cast out demons,
then the kingdom of God has come upon you" (See Matthew 12:28). Again see
Luke 16:16 and its corresponding verse in Matthew 11:12-13. The implication
again is that the kingdom of God is actually present. Again see Luke 17:20-21.
When asked by the Pharisees when the kingdom of God was coming, Jesus
answered to them that the kingdom of God is not coming; "the kingdom of God
is in the midst of you."

In the Gospel of John the kingdom of God is not mentioned, with the exception of 3:3 and 3:5. "In general . . . this evangelist has reinterpreted the teaching
of Jesus so that instead of speaking of the kingdom of God he speaks of eternal
life or life."[11] From many passages it is clear that John thought that eternal life
or life is a present possession. In John 5:24 we read: "Truly, truly, I say to you,
he who hears my word and believes him who sent me, has eternal life; he does not
come into judgment, but has passed from death to life." (See also John 3:10-21,
31-32; 5:24; 6:47, 53-54; 17:3.) This theme of eternal life as a present possession is
reiterated in the letter of John: "God gave us eternal life and this life is his Son.
He who has the Son has life" (I John 5:11-12). Indeed John writes his letter that
his readers will know that they "have eternal life" (I John 5:13).

Thirdly, we may take the view that the kingdom will come in the future, but
this event is further in the future than was believed by proponents of the first
view. Meanwhile we have something present as a reality in our midst, that is, the
fellowship of the Holy Spirit at whose coming the Church was created. This
Church, reflecting the finished work of God in Christ, is a present reality. It
foreshadows the kingdom to come. It is, we may say, the inauguration of the
kingdom, the final establishment of what will come in the end.

This third view is, I think, the predominant view of the author of
Luke—Acts. Luke addresses himself to this problem, the delay of the coming of
this kingdom of Christ. The account by Luke in Acts leads from Jerusalem, the
place of Jesus' passion, along Paul's missionary journeys to Rome, the place of
Paul's martyrdom. This author was concerned with the problem of getting on
with Rome during this indefinite interim.

He has a sense of salvation or sacred history, and this is a major emphasis in this work. His account of salvation history is divided into four periods.[12] There is, first, the time of the law and the prophets, from Adam to John the Baptist; secondly, the time of proclamation by Jesus to his crucifixion; thirdly, the period of resurrection and revelatory teaching to the ascension; fourthly, the time of proclamation in the interim between the birth of the Church at Pentecost to the establishment of the kingdom in God's time.

I have described the structure of this interim, as developed of mature senses of remembrance, expectation, waiting, working, and hoping. For his part Luke gives a worldwide structure for the work to be done: "But you shall receive power when the Holy Spirit has come upon you; and you shall be my witnesses in Jerusalem and in all Judea and Samaria and to the end of the earth" (Acts 1:9).

In this work of mine with emphasis on sacred history and the development of personal maturity I am naturally inclined to take the third of these three views—that one reflected in Luke—Acts. In this compromise view, we have the fivefold character of the sacred historical moment still intact. To grow in the maturity of Christ during this interim is to develop each of the five aspects of the character of this interim time. To grow is to refresh our memories by continued study. The study will take a distinctive form; it will be the retelling of the story. It will be a continual rehearsal of the sacred historical story of the moments from the beginning to the moment of Jesus Christ. It will be continued application of the moments in this story to the process of becoming mature. By such rehearsals we will be following the example of the people of God in their sacred histories at such moments as the covenant renewal ceremony in Joshua Chapter twenty-four and the pronouncement of the Deuteronomic Confession of Faith as stated in Deuteronomy (Deuteronomy 26:5-9).

This increased awareness of our sacred history will enliven our sense of expectation, and, so, in this way also we will be growing in the maturity of Christ. We will wait, knowing that the time of the coming of the kingdom is not ours to determine. It is not for us "to know times or seasons which the Father has fixed" (Acts 1:7). In our waiting, we "shall receive power when the Holy Spirit has come upon . . ." us, and we will be his witnesses in our worlds. We will be growing in our spirit-filled time of waiting and working, and this will enliven and enrich our hoping for the coming of the Kingdom of God.

In the end, in the final consummation of sacred history, the kingdom of God will come and be established and all the promises of God will be fulfilled. God in Christ, finally, will be Lord of all history. Again, as in the beginning, we will have unbroken communion with God and with each other in the world. What will this end be like?

Firstly, the kingdom of God is a new creation. The old world will pass away and be destroyed; "The heavens will pass away with a loud noise, and the elements will be dissolved with fire, and the earth and the works that are upon it will be burned up" (2 Peter 3:10). Or "the earth will wear out like a garment, and they who dwell in it will die like gnats" (Isaiah 51:6). According to his promise it is thus a new creation for which we wait, and this is reminiscent of the prophecies of Isaiah: "For behold, I create new heavens and a new earth" (Isaiah 55:17; See also Isaiah 66:22).

This act of a new creation by the Lord God we have seen over and over again in our rehearsal of the sacred historical story and in our developing maturity. We saw it in the creation of the world in the beginning. We saw it in the creation of the resurrected Jesus and of the fellowship of the Holy Spirit, which we call the Church.

The emphasis here on a new creation is distinctly different from a conception of the world being renewed and transformed. We found this latter emphasis in the Noah moment when the world was washed clean. Such a transformation was not accepted by the Lord God after the fact, however. He said after the flood that he would "never again curse the ground" or "destroy every living creature as I have done" (Genesis 8:12). "While the earth remains, seedtime and harvest, cold and heat, summer and winter, day and night, shall not cease" (Genesis 8:22). The emphasis there on the times that the earth remains suggests that the time is limited. In the end the earth remains no more, and the new age dawns with the creation of a new world.

We have seen so far that the end will be a new creation. Will there be a second coming at the end to usher in the coming of the kingdom? That there will be a coming was surely believed. "For the Lord himself will descend from heaven with a cry of command, with the archangel's call, and with the sound of the trumpet of God" (I Thessalonians 4:16). (See also Matthew 24:30-31; Mark 13:26-27 and I Corinthians 15:52.) With the exception of Hebrews 9:28, "the phrase (second coming) does not occur in the New Testament, which omits 'second', e.g. Matt. 24:3; I Thess. 2:19; Jas. 5:7; II Pet. 3:4."[13]

So the coming of the kingdom in the end will be ushered in by a coming of Christ, at which time "the dead in Christ will rise first" (I Thessalonians 4:16b). According to the Revelation to John, events will occur as follows. The conquering Christ will come (Revelation 19:11-16). He comes on a white horse and is called Faithful and True, "and the name by which he is called is the Word of God . . . On his robe and on his thigh he has a name inscribed, King of kings and Lord of lords" (Revelation 19:16). He will achieve victory over the beast, the Antichrist (Revelation 19:17-21). Satan will be overcome, and bound, his rule of the present evil age being suspended for the millennium (20:1-3). During this millennium Christ will rule with the martyrs, those faithful in Christ who have been asleep, and who have been resurrected by the conquering Christ in the first resurrection.

Following the millennium "Satan will be loosed from his prison and will come out to deceive the nations . . ." (Revelation 20:7-8), which are represented by Gog and Magog. The deceived nations will be defeated and Satan will be cast into the lake of fire, ending the present age of the world. At this time, at the time of the coming of the kingdom of God, there will be a second resurrection and a general and final judgment (Revelation 20:11-15), which is depicted in Revelation as follows:

> Then I saw a great white throne and him who sat upon it; from his presence earth and sky fled away, and no place was found for them. And I saw the dead, great and small, standing before the throne, and books were opened. Also another book was opened, which is the book of life. And the dead were judged by what was written in the books, by what they had done. And the sea gave up the dead in it, Death and Hades gave up the dead in them, and all were judged by what they had done. Then Death and Hades were thrown into the lake of fire. This

is the second death, the lake of fire; and if any one's name was not found written in the book of life, he was thrown into the lake of fire.

At the coming of Christ the dead will rise (I Thessalonians 4:16b), and according to the Revelation of John, they, the martyrs, will rule with Christ during the millennium. Christ had been the first born of the dead at his resurrection, and those faithful in Christ, the martyrs, have, during the interim before the resurrection, been asleep.

What the end is like, whenever it comes, is depicted in the 21st and 22nd Chapter of The Revelation to John. The dwelling place in the kingdom of God will be the new Jerusalem, newly created by God. Why is the kingdom created anew called a "new Jerusalem"? Recall that Jerusalem was the city of David, in which was realized the promise of God to Abraham that there would be a nation by which all the families of the earth shall bless themselves. Recall also the prophecies of Isaiah that there shall come forth a "shoot from the stump of Jesse," upon whom the spirit of the Lord will rest. That prophecy was fulfilled in Jesus the Christ who was crucified, who died and who rose again in Jerusalem.

In the new Jerusalem God will dwell with the people, "and they shall be his people, and God himself will be with them" (Revelation 21:3). Every tear will be wiped from our eyes, "and death shall be no more, neither shall there be mourning nor crying nor pain any more, for the former things have passed away" (Revelation 21:4).

Our heavenly kingdom will have a radiance in God's glory "like a most rare jewel, like a jasper, clear as crystal" (Revelation 21:11). There is no sun or moon to shine upon this city, "for the glory of God is its light, and its lamp is the Lamb" (Revelation 21:23). Neither is there a temple or Church, "for its temple is the Lord God the Almighty and the Lamb" (Revelation 21:22).

In this kingdom of God we are to live as God intended us to live, in a state of utter dependence on him. This self-insufficiency is to be our final maturity. So he is our light and the object of our worship and adoration. Also he is the water of life for which we have longed. "As a hart longs for flowing streams, so longs my soul for thee, O God. My soul thirsts for God, for the living God" (Psalm 42:1). "For waters shall break forth in the wilderness, and streams in the desert; the burning sand shall become a pool, and the thirsty ground springs of water" (Isaiah 35:6b and 7a). He shows us "the river of the water of life, bright as crystal, flowing from the throne of God and of the Lamb through the middle of the street of the city . . ." (Revelation 22:1-2). On either side of the river there are trees of life. It was the fruit of this tree which we were denied in the Garden in the beginning. We were expelled from the Garden, lest, having become little gods for ourselves, we would reach out and eat of the fruit of the tree of life and live forever. (See Ezekiel 47:4-12 for further imagery of trees by the side of the river of life.)

Now, however, the trees of life yield fruit, one for each month of the year, sufficient to meet all our needs. Our heavenly father knows our needs. In his kingdom all these things are ours. (See Matthew 6:32-33.)

There is a real sense in which the end is like the beginning. In our sacred historical story, and in the story of our developing maturity, in both the beginning and the end, we are to live in a state of absolute dependence upon him. In the end all the problems raised by the succumbing to the temptations to be little gods knowing good and evil for ourselves will be overcome. We will, once again, be faithful creatures of God. In the new Jerusalem we will have found the kingdom of God and his righteousness, and our lives will be lived, once again, in unbroken communion with God in Christ.

10

Appendix:
The Historicist Perspective

From the extended rehearsal of the sacred historical story there emerges the process of becoming a Biblical Christian and that of becoming personally mature. This we have seen. What also emerges from within the rehearsal is a perspective, which I call "historicist." In the rehearsal of Biblical history it becomes clear that the whole Biblical story may be expressed in historical terms. So also in historical terms does a person understand himself, his relation to God, and God himself. Even the world is understood historically, for it is but that in which God is working out his purposes in history. "Historicist" is a name which may be given to the outlook by which everything that exists is viewed exclusively in historical terms. This perspective also provides a proper basis for philosophical and theological conclusions about Biblical Christianity. In this Appendix I wish to discuss this perspective and these conclusions.

A. The Historicist Perspective and Historicism
The central claim of the historicist perspective is that everything that exists is viewed exclusively in historical terms. In this work on Biblical Christianity, what exists is God, man and the world. These realities are understood to be thoroughly historical. By this claim is meant that there is no real part of ourselves or of the world that is not historical, that there is no knowable part of God that is not historical, that our relationship with God is exclusively historical, found, that is, in sacred history.

To adopt the historicist perspective is to adopt the historicist point of view of these realities. This is the position to which we are being led in our rehearsal of the moments of the sacred historical story. This is a position to be taken by the Biblical Christian who relies exclusively on the movement of sacred history as that is given us in the Bible. This work is a proposal in thought, as I said at the end of the Introduction in Section 1. We have yet to see in this Appendix whether historicism provides an enlightening perspective for viewing Biblical Christianity.

Maurice Mandelbaum formulates a definition of 'historicism,' as follows: "Historicism is the belief that an adequate understanding of the nature of anything and an adequate assessment of its value are to be gained by considering it in terms of the place it occupied and the role it played within a process of development."[1] Mandelbaum goes on to note that "this definition does not characterize historicism as a particular *Weltanschauung* but as a methodological belief concerning explanation and evaluation."[2] Historicism is characterized this way, thinks Mandelbaum, because of so many divergencies between the points of view of the various historicist thinkers.

F. L. Baumer shows that the prevailing idea in the historicist outlook was relativism. As the historian Morley said, historicism meant "the triumph of the

91

principle of relativity in historic judgment, . . . the substitution of becoming for being, the relative for the absolute, dynamic movement for dogmatic immobility."[3] It meant, comments Baumer, "referring everything, men's ideas and beliefs included, to its origins, understanding it in terms of its historical milieu."[4]

In precisely what sense is the historicist perspective an historicism? Its roots lie not in the culture, not in any mix of intellectual, social and national conditions in any particular time and place. It is especialy clear that its roots do not lie either in a philosophical tradition, such as Hegelianism. Its roots lie, rather, in the movement of sacred history from moment to moment in the relationship between God and man. To be sure, man who has a sacred historical relationship with God is man set within particular cultures in specific times and places. Over the course of sacred history, to be sure, there have been many changing general historical circumstances. It is not to these, however, that the sacred historian, or the Biblical Christian, turns for guidance. He looks, rather, to the movement of sacred history itself, from moment to moment, and not to changing and relative cultural conditions in which the Biblical characters lived. Our characterization of the sacred historical moments, and the dynamic relation between them, has been a characterization of a reality independent of relativistic cultural circumstances.

What Morley said about historicism in general does apply to the historicist perspective. This viewpoint unabashedly is concerned with "becoming" rather than with "being," with "dynamic movement" rather than "dogmatic immobility." Insofar as our understanding of the nature of God, man and the world are all to be understood in terms of dynamic process, we have substituted the relative for the absolute. We admitted as much when we adopted the strategy of translation of Biblical Christian language of sacred history into the language referring to personal maturity.

The historicist perspective is an historicism also in a sense suggested by Mandelbaum. For this work it is the case that the nature of everything, of God, man and the world, and the value of these are gained by considering them in terms of the place that they occupied and the role that they have played in a process of development. The "process of development" for this work is the unfolding of the sacred historical story. And the dynamic unfolding of the moments of sacred history is a "methodological belief concerning explanation and evaluation." Insofar as the movement of sacred history is seen to be authoritative for the Biblical Christian, it serves as a methodological principle. It shows us what we know of God, of ourselves, of the world, and it shows us how we know these things.

The historicist perspective is a *Weltanschauung*, or world view, one with ontological commitments concerning the existents—God, man and the world. It is based on the movement of sacred history, and as such shows us some limitations of man's understanding of the nature of God, man and the world. The setting of these limitations is one of the most helpful consequences of this viewpoint.

Is the historicist perspective a metaphysic? In discussing the nature of metaphysics W. H. Walsh notes "three main features of metaphysics as traditionally practiced."[5] "It claims to tell us what really exists or what the real nature of things is, it claims to be fundamental and comprehensive in a way in which no individual science is, and it claims to reach conclusions which are intellectually impregnable and thus possess a unique kind of certainty."[6] If we accept the characterization of the historicist perspective as a world view, we would seem to be engaging in a work of metaphysics. Each of the three of Walsh's features of traditional metaphysics will be examined to see if this is so.

In the first place, the historicist perspective does not claim to tell what exists nor does it adequately and systematically explain what the real nature of a thing is. The guiding principle behind this entire work is that every conclusion to be drawn about Biblical Christianity is to be based exclusively on the rehearsal of the moments in the sacred historical story.

In the telling of that story it has been assumed that God is, that man is and that the world is. It is assumed that man and God have a relationship, and that the world is a stage on which this relationship is carried out. Metaphysical systems may also have assumptions, but the nature of the things assumed to exist are rationally justified entirely within the system, which is, therefore, shown to be consistent. Such rational justification is not part of the telling of a story.

On the basis of the rehearsal of the sacred historical story there will be philosophical conclusions drawn out about the nature of each of the three realities assumed to exist in the story. As noted above particular attention will be given to the drawing of limitations of the understanding we have of the natures of God, man and the world. The conclusions drawn will not give a developed metaphysical theory about the natures of whatever exists. There will be no explanation of these natures within a consistent system. The conclusions will be of the order of sign posts or indications of general characteristics of their natures and especially of the limitations of our understanding of these natures. When I say "limitations of our understanding" I mean that the Biblical Christian is limited in his understanding of the nature of God, man and the world, limited to what he experiences, the dynamic movement of sacred history in himself.

The second and third of Walsh's characteristics of metaphysics may be treated together. The historicist perspective does claim to be fundamental, but only so as a perspective for understanding and applying Biblical Christianity as it is. The historicist perspective is not taken in this work to be fundamental in the way that metaphysics traditionally has been taken. Metaphysics has been considered fundamental in the sense that it provides a systematic theoretical and comprehensive foundation on the basis of which all the individual sciences or disciplines may be understood. The theoretical foundation has been thought to be "impregnable" in the sense that it often has been based on logical argumentation, especially deduction. For example, the system of Descartes and that of Spinoza started with what were taken to be intuitively certain axioms or propositions from which logically certain consequences are deduced. This is the unique kind of certainty possessed by a metaphysical system. In the historicist perspective there is no such certainty.

In this Appendix there will be no general defense of the philosophy of historicism. I have adopted this point of view in order to understand Biblical Christianity. I have argued that there is a process of development within sacred history as that is found in the Bible. I do not, however, claim to step outside this dynamic historical process to attempt to justify the philosophy of historicism. That would be to seek to give it the metaphysical foundations I have just denied that it has as a basis for Biblical Christianity. It may be that no such rational defense is possible. It may be that historicism is as standpoint simply taken or assumed. In this work the argument follows but does not precede the taking of this stand. The argument here is that given this point of view Biblical Christianity may be understood in a fresh and insightful way.

B. The Authoritative Movement of Sacred History

To adopt the historicist perspective is, among other commitments, to adopt an authority in Biblical Christianity. Traditionally such authorities have been conceived as the Bible, reason, experience, and the Church. According to the historicist perspective, the final authority, more basic than any of these four traditionally conceived authorities, is the movement of sacred history. Gordon Kaufman, in his systematic theology, gives a lead: "The ultimate arbiter of theological validity is not reason or experience or the Bible or the church, but the movement of history itself—understood theologically: the providence of God."[7]

What is authoritative, following Kaufman's lead, is the movement of sacred history from moment to moment, from season of the spirit to season, which is the final arbiter of any question concerning Biblical Christianity. The Bible in the main is a record of this sacred history. In any question of Biblical faith, or the application of the Bible to a practical situation, we are to look to the movement of this sacred history as a basis for our answer. As Kaufman states: "It is this movement which in actual fact sorts out the valid from the invalid, the significant from the insignificant."[8] In the historicist perspective it is to the movement of history that one looks to understand man, man's relation to God, God himself, and God's world.

In our rehearsal of the sacred historical story, when we attended to the movement of sacred history, we learned of what it is for God in Christ to be Lord. Our final authority is that through which the Biblical Christian may learn of the Lordship of God in Christ, and we find this in the sacred historical relationship God has with man. We look through the Pentateuch and the Law, through the historical accounts, the prophets and the writings including Psalms, through the revelation to the moments in the sacred historical story. In any matter of understanding the Biblical message, or seeking guidance for some practical concern, we ask ourselves how one or more of these moments, or repetitive patterns between them, informs us of how we are to believe and act. To attend to these movements enables us to sort out the significant from the insignificant and enables us to keep a clear eye on the Lordship of God in Christ.

That the Bible is a record of the sacred historical movement implies that the movement itself is distinct from the Bible. The Bible indicates how God, who is real, relates to us who are real, and the dynamic movement is a reality attested to by the scriptures. In one sense this is particularly clear, for it can be said that the Bible is a record of the sacred historical relation between man and God that is not complete. What is told there is on-going now in extra-Biblical times, including our own. The sacred history has been unfolding, and it will unfold under the providence of God. This unfolding is a dynamic reality distinct from the Bible itself, and as Biblical Christians, for whom God in Christ is Lord, it is this which is authoritative.

We have been considering only one of the four candidates for the final authority as indicated by Kaufman, that is, the Bible. He also mentions reason, experience and the Church. I wish to consider each of these. If reason were the final authority for the Biblical Christian, then the tests he would bring to each decision in his life would be rational. We would naturally, therefore, ask whether a certain source of action would "make sense" or whether it would be consistent with what has been done, or was called for, in the past. We are seeing, however, as we are reviewing the sacred historical story, that such rational questions as these were not asked, nor were there discussions based upon such questions as these.

From first to last it must be remembered what the motivating question of this study is for the Biblical Christian. What is it for God in Christ to be Lord? If the tests by which he decides any given course of action are rational, then God is not Lord, for he is making the rational decision as to whether what he calls us to do coheres with our own rational standards.

A similar point can be made about experience as the "ultimate arbiter of theological validity." It may be said that what or how one feels is and should be authoritative for that person. It may be said that the Biblical Christian would not act unless and until he feels a certain way, special to him. On this point of view it should be said directly that in one sense how one feels is irrelevant. If God in Christ is Lord, if he calls the Biblical Christian to do x then it does not make any difference how he feels. What makes the difference is that the spirit of God is or is not upon that Biblical figure. As with the authority of reason, the authority of man's experience makes man his own Lord and not God in Christ.

To say that the movement of sacred history has an authority prior to that of the Church is included within this sacred historical movement. It can be argued that the Church should be that vehicle which lives under the Lordship of God in Christ in sacred history and which helps others to do the same. In an extensive treatment of liturgy in *Theological Dimensions of the Liturgy* Don Cyprian Vagaggini shows how the liturgy of the Church manifests "the great phases" of sacred history.[9] According to this way of thinking moments of the sacred historical story would then be reflected in the movement of the liturgy throughout the Church year.

One of the consequences of adopting the historicist perspective is that the Biblical Christian will regard sacred history and not general history as of the greatest importance. In comparison to the importance of sacred history and the lessons to be learned from it, the significance of general history simply pales. This is not to deny that there is a general history, as some may think. The historicist perspective is a vehicle for putting first things first in Biblical Christianity and relegating all other things to their proper level of importance.

C. The Nature of God

In the historicist perspective the Biblical Christian understands and experiences God himself in sacred history. I have shown that in the moments of the sacred historical story there is a progressive revelation of God. God reveals himself to man in history. What is known of God is known only in history. In Jesus the Christ, who became man, and who dwelt among man, and in whom all the previous moments in the sacred historical story are fulfilled, man knows all that there is to know about God. As the historicist perspective has it this knowledge is exclusively historical, that is, exclusively within sacred history.

To determine what specific knowledge man does in fact have of God we may ask the following question: what can one know of God in sacred history, which knowledge can be stated in historical terms exclusively? By determining the knowledge of God that is had in sacred history the Biblical Christian will be defining precisely the limits of man's knowledge of God and of his nature.

To claim that God is to be viewed in historical terms only would be to hold the view that there is nothing knowable in or of God which is not itself historical, that is, which cannot be stated in historical terms exclusively. Can this claim about knowledge of God be supported? To determine this, one needs to apply the test question by asking what is it that man knows of God in history. It then has to be determined what problems, if any that there are if knowledge of God's nature is strictly limited to such historical knowledge.

In his book entitled *Philosophy of Religion* John Hick devotes his first Chapter to a discussion of the "Judaic-Christian Concept of God."[10] Specifically, he discusses the traditional "attributes" or characteristics of God's nature. The basic idea, he says, is that God is infinite or unlimited. In this infinity are the traditional ideas of God as omnipotent (infinitely powerful), omnipresent (unlimited in space and time), and omniscient (unlimited in knowledge). He also is thought to be self-existent, ". . . not dependent either for existence or for characteristics upon any reality."[11] It follows that he is eternal, interpreted by Anselm to mean "absolutely outside all time."[12] Moreover, God is conceived of as a "self-existent Creator," creating the world "out of nothing."[13] God is personal. He is a God of goodness, love and grace, which Hick thinks ". . . are all virtually synonymous, and the most characteristic of the three terms is love."[14] "The infinite divine love . . . gives rise to that side of religious experience in which God is known as claiming the total obedience of a man's life. God is thought of as 'Lord' and 'King' as well as 'Father.' "[15] Being personal, God also exemplifies "wrath" and judgment. Finally, God is Holy. Hick's own summary of "The 'Judaic-Christian Concept of God' is as follows: God is conceived as the infinite, eternal, uncreated, personal reality, who has created all that exists and who is revealed to human creatures as holy and loving."[16]

What do these attributes mean? I will consider the first group together, namely infinity, self-existent, eternal, absolute creator. In his sacred historical experience in relation to God how does the Biblical Christian know that God has these "metaphysical attributes"? The gist of the answer is that he cannot know them by definition of the terms in which these characteristics are expressed. For God to reveal his infinitude would be for him to enter the finite, which the Biblical Christian believes, of course, that he has done. Entering into the finite requires historical change, which the infinite as such does not. In this sense infinity implies unchangeableness. So the belief is that God becomes historical only insofar as he enters into the finite. Insofar as he does not enter into the finite he may be said to be infinite, but, of course, that is not something man knows or can know in his sacred historical relation with God, for such relation is in the finite.

This kind of argument about infinite would exactly parallel arguments on the other metaphysical attributes. The Biblical Christian knows that he depends on God, not on God's self-existence. Knowledge of God is in sacred history, not eternity. The eternal, implying the uncreated, is to be distinguished from the immortal, which I take to mean created but undestroyed. The Biblical Christian knows his dependency on God, but not that he is absolute creator. To have been created, for him, means only that he has been given all the conditions for having a sacred historical relationship with God.

Within the moments of the sacred historical story what man knows is the appearance of things. That things are created or come to be means simply that they appear. Thus in the beginning of his sacred historical relation to God there is a world. He knows the world, he knows a system of appearances that are relatively constant and relatively coherent, but he does not know its coming to be. He knows only its appearance. He knows the resurrection body of Jesus, the transformed body, which simply appears before him, and he knows not its creation. He knows the fellowship created by the Holy Spirit, but he knows not its origin. In these instances what man knows in his sacred historical relation with God is what appears, that is what is created by God for him to acknowledge God as Lord.

What does the Biblical Christian know of God's personal characteristics, those of goodness, love and grace, together with God thought of as Lord, King and Father, who may be wrathful or judgmental? Of these attributes he who is in sacred historical relation with God knows much indeed. It is abundantly evident in the rehearsal just what these characteristics come to. So, the goodness of God was, for example, in the appearances of manna and quail for the people to eat in the wilderness. The love of God and his grace appeared repeatedly, as for example, in God's intervention in the Abrahamic moment when the knife was poised ready for the plunge into Isaac. God appeared as King in David and in Jesus the Christ. God the Father, has been evident throughout in constant, even undeserved, care. God the wrathful and judgmental appeared to the people who murmured against him unfaithfully in the wilderness. It has been my contention in the rehearsal of the moments of the sacred historical story we learn what it is for God in Christ to be Lord.

Finally, what does it mean to say that God is Holy? In the moment of Moses and the Exodus, God, the Holy One, appeared to Moses on the mountain in Exodus Chapter 3. He appeared also to Isaiah in the temple in Isaiah, Chapter 6. When asked his name by Moses, God responded, "I am who I am." We asked what kind of name this was. God, the Holy One, is identifying himself as the one who is, who will be what he will be, who will cause to happen what he causes to happen. In such an identification it is not possible for the Biblical Christian to know who he is, or what he will be or what he will cause to happen unless he reveals it to him. Thus the house was filled with smoke and the Lord God was enthroned, high and lifted up, present to Isaiah, yet hidden. God, the Holy, does not reveal himself to man directly.

To say that God has the attribute of holiness means that in one's sacred historical relation to God there are Moses-on-the-mountain moments or Isaiah-in-the-temple moments, in which God appears, but also in which God remains hidden as in a great mystery. In these moments one has the sense of being filled with awe. To say that God is Holy is to say this and not one sentence more.

By considering the traditional attributes of God's nature I have shown how proper limitations may be drawn. Within Biblical Christianity the relevant principle is as follows: man's knowledge of God and of his nature is limited to what man experiences in his sacred historical relation to God. Doctrines about God's nature about which there is no light shed in sacred history, such as the self-existence of God, may properly be dismissed as speculative. According to the historicist perspective God is an historical being with whom man relates in sacred history.

Man's knowledge of God is found in his sacred historical relationship with him and only in such.

D. The Historicity of Man and Life After Death

After the crucifixion Jesus was dead, really dead, and he was buried. This shows Jesus' full humanity. From this event we also are introduced to an idea central to the historicist perspective, that is that man is to be understood exclusively in historical terms. For Kaufman this means that "man is a thoroughly historical being."[17] Man's consciousness is thoroughly historical, "all that we experience and understand is shaped by the ideas and language that structure our consciousness, and this speech and thought are themselves in continuous historical process."[18] In this work the continuous historical process is found in the movement of sacred history. Repeatedly in the rehearsal of the moments in this sacred historical process I have claimed that the fully developed Biblical Christian is seen in the development of the seasons of the spirit, that is, in the moments of sacred history. Corresponding to these seasons are the moments in the development of the fully mature life. This claim has been supported as we have shown how the life of faith, as that is given in the Bible, necessarily includes the full cycle of the sacred historical moments, not only moments of success and unity as in the season of David, but also spiritual seasons of despair and seeming loss of hope as in the fall of Jerusalem and exile moments.

For Kaufman, the theologian, the historicity of man shows us how we may best understand the traditional idea of the image of God, in which man is created. Recall the beginning moments in which "the Lord God formed man of dust from the ground, and breathed into his nostrils the breath of life; and man became a living being" (Genesis 2:7). Kaufman comments: "Human history has . . . (a) special significance because in it another historical being in addition to God appears and begins to work out his own purposes, thus creating further history."[19] Man, according to his point of view, is intrinsically historical, like God in history. To say that man is created in the image of God means that man, like God, works out his purposes in history, and thus, like God, he himself creates further history. Thus is man created in the image of God. Thus again is the special significance of man, who is historical to his roots.

To say that man is historical is to enter the arenas of metaphysics and the philosophy of mind, for to make such a claim is to say something about man's nature. Within these areas we find various competing theories of the self or person. There are two theories of special relevance to this work. One, which I call the soul view, is relevant because it has been taken widely to be Biblical and yet in a strong sense it denies the historicity of man. The other, a materialist view, is relevant because, as I will argue, it is Biblical, and in a strong sense it affirms the historicity of man. A critical analysis of these two theories will help to explain just what it is and what it is not for man to be thoroughly historical. I will argue that the materialist view best illustrates the historicity of man for the Biblical Christian.

The soul view is clearly contrary to a view of man which holds that man is "thoroughly historical," for it is the view which claims that there is an ahistorical part or dimension of man, something in and of man which is implicitly immortal or even eternal. It is something called a soul.

The real person, or better yet, what is the really important part of the person, is identified with a soul, or mind, or spirit. For purposes of this work these terms, 'soul,' 'mind,' or 'spirit,' may be used interchangeably. The body is an outer garment, as it were, a prison house, which is part of the person to be sure, but which restricts the free activity of the soul. Desires and temptations of the person, having their seat within the body, tend to break up the harmony of the soul, to disrupt the peace and stillness, to lead the person into a state of confusion.

Essentially the soul is an unchanging thing, a spiritual entity, which is the same self or person through changes in time. For Plato the soul was eternal. For the supposedly Christian doctrine of the immortality of the soul it is implicitly immortal, being created by God and being destined to live forever. While we live, while the soul is imprisoned, it is related to something else, the body, essentially alien to it. The relation of soul and body is potentially self-destructive for the soul.

The relation of soul and body is emphasized by Descartes, another classical exponent of this view. For Descartes the relation was called interaction, which essentially is a two-way causal efficacy. States, events and processes in the body have their effects in the body. The body and soul each are real distinguishable existent things or substances. The soul is a spiritual nonphysical entity, nonphysical in the sense that it has no physical properties whatsoever. For example, it has no mass, or for Descartes, no extension. The other real thing or substance is a physical body with, for example, mass and extension. The soul or mind has its seat within the body, and it interacts with it.

The view of life after death which is the companion to the soul view is called the immortality of the soul view. Death is, accordingly, the great liberator. At "death" the soul, which is implicitly immortal by nature, is loosed from the prisonhouse of the body to return to its eternal home or to find its natural resting place with God. To say that the soul is implicitly immortal is just to claim, as was done above, that the soul has no physical properties. Physical properties are such that they change, or decay, or "die." Such death does occur to the body, and so, in the immortality of the soul view, the death of a person really is only the death of the body. Death is only the dissolution of the material body, the effects of which disturb the mental and spiritual peace of the soul.

With this kind of a picture given by the immortality of the soul view, it can been seen that the "death" of Socrates, which is based on the belief not only in immortality but also the eternality of the soul, stands in sharp contrast to the death of Jesus. Socrates, in typical fashion, argues that the soul is immortal, that is, that it is not subject to decay or destruction. Having convinced himself of this, he dies in the peaceful knowledge that his soul will be freed from his body, freed to enjoy the peaceful harmony which he, the philosopher, has only glimpsed. How different this view is from the death of Jesus as that was described in Section 8.C.

The second view among these competing theories is one which I will call the Biblical materialist view. Accordingly, man is an organic unity, a living body. There is nothing to man, to the human person, except the vital living body. We can speak of the soul on this view, but we are to understand by 'soul' the principle of life or vitality in the body. The soul is not a substantial spiritual and separable entity, able, as it were, to live on its own. Man is conceived as an organic unity, an animated body. That this view is a sort of materialism is shown by the fact that all talk of persons is body talk. In other words there is on this view nothing to man except the vital living body. In contemporary language this statement would come down to the claim that everything about a person can be explained by reference to states, events or processes in the body, particularly the brain and central nervous system. On this view we may say that people do not have bodies; they are animated bodies.

In the Biblical Old Testament imagery these bodily states and processes are thought of as breath. God breathed into the dust of the ground the breath of life. Man breathes and he lives. "In Genesis 6:17, God tells Noah that he will bring a flood upon the earth to destroy all . . . (basar), flesh, and he describes it as all which has in it . . . (ruach chayim) the spirit of life. And in Genesis 7:22 both terms are joined in describing living creatures, 'All in whom are (neshmat ruach chayim), the breath and the spirit of life.' "[20]

Levi A. Olan notes in his book called *Judaism and Immortality* that the soul was conceived in early Biblical thought to be a "function of the material body when quickened by spirit."[21] The soul is identified not only with breath but also with blood. Leviticus states that the "life of the flesh is in the blood" (Leviticus 17:11). "The law prohibiting the eating of meat which retains the blood also reflects this viewpoint."[22] Death is seen as a leaving of the body by the spirit or life. This means nothing more than this: man breathes his last, and the blood dries up.

In the New Testament references are made to spirit and soul but mostly in Paul to spirit. In Paul this is contrasted to flesh. Transliterated, the relevant words in Paul are 'psyche'—soul; 'pheuma'—spirit; 'soma'—flesh, and 'nepesh'—soul or life principle. In certain of the infrequent uses of 'soul' Paul sometimes means the natural or unspiritual man. He never means to suggest that there is a dualism of soul and body. 'Spirit' is a term used mainly to refer to God or to incorporeal beings, such as angels. Especially in Paul it means the divine element in human personality.

There are four difficulties with the soul view of the person and its companion, the doctrine of the immortality of the soul, which render it untenable. In the first place, there is the problem of personal identity, personal identity both in this life and between this life and life after death. According to the soul view what gives one a personal identity is the continuity of one's soul.

On this point the philosopher Terrence Penelhum writes convincingly in terms of a mental or spiritual substance.

> Historically this notion (of spiritual substance) has served dualistically minded philosophers as a means of providing continuous ownership for the sequences of thoughts and feelings that make up men's mental lives . . . . Since the concept of substance is not an empirical one, there is no publicly usable set of devices for determining the continued presence of a substance, so its presence cannot serve as a criterion for applying the expression "the same person" in ordinary life . . . . (n)o content seems available for the doctrine . . . . (T)he doctrine amounts to no more than a pious assurance that all is well, deep down. It provides no reason for this assurance.[23]

The major thrust of Penelhum's argument, I take it, is the claim that the concept of soul is not an empirical one. This is to claim that as a matter of psychological fact man does not experience the soul as such whenever he enters into what he calls his self. As Hume argued, we always are impressed by or perceive some particular perception or other, of light or shade, love or hatred. We never catch ourselves distinct from some such perception.[24] If we do, as a matter of act, experience the soul which endures through time, what would be experienced would be the same or be constant. But, argues Hume, there is no one constant impression. Thus there is no empirical content to the claim that what makes me the same person throughout life and the same person in the afterlife is the continuity of my soul.

A second difficulty is the problem of individuation: how can one individuate one soul from another? On the soul view the soul is a real thing separable from the body. It is, therefore, capable of surviving and living in a disembodied state. In such a disembodied state, however, how do we individuate one soul from another? Normally persons are distinguished by distinguishing between their bodies. One knows that another person is in the room, for example, because his body can be seen and by this he can be distinguished from other persons. Without the availability of another's body how could any other person be individuated?

As an aspect of both the personal identity problem and the individuation problem can be isolated as the third problem for maximum destructive effect. According to the soul view, a person is a body and a soul or mind in interaction. At death the soul is freed from the confines of the body. It follows that what survives death is a mental or spiritual remnant of the person, no longer an individual in its own right and no longer the same person as before death. On the immortality of the soul view it is not the whole of man which is freed, but rather only a part of man, even if it is his most important part, the soul, which has been imprisoned within the body.

A fourth difficulty can be seen in the very idea of a disembodied surviving life. Without a body or bodily organs of perception and sensation what kind of life would it be? Without a body would there be any sense at all in which one could be said to see, hear, touch or act? Actions of a person would necessarily be restricted to those which could be engaged in by a soul, a surviving remnant of the person. Insofar as the power of individuation of other persons is questionable at best, such a life would apparently be very lonely. Whether or not the immortality of the soul view is acceptable is in part dependent on this conception of a surviving life.

In *Survival and Disembodied Existence* Penelhum considers "Disembodied Existence and Perception" in Chapter Two and "Disembodied Agency" in Chapter Three.[25] In order for a disembodied person to be correctly able to see, Penelhum argues that he would have to be in space. But the soul is defined in such a way that it fills no part of space. Nonetheless, Penelhum thinks that there is no good reason to deny the disembodied person a visual field in which there are images. But, argues Penelhum, without organs of perceptions he would not be able to attain to adequate assurance on how things actually were to anything like the extent to which an embodied person can."[26]

Without organs or perception it is difficult to understand how a disembodied person could be said to correct his perceptions. An analogous point is made by Penelhum about emotions and attitudes, which "would run the risk of being ill-founded to the extent to which his information about the world is inadequate."[27] What about disembodied agency and action? All of us have to do certain things in order, for example, to move our hands and arms in order to move the table. "In the case of the disembodied agent there must be some analogue of this, and this will be the mental act of willing."[28]

Since Gilbert Ryle on *The Concept of Mind* the philosophical community has had enough trouble explaining acts of the will in this life. In the next life the occult or magical character of this phenomenon would be heightened even further. Enough has been said, I think, to cast doubt on the kind of life consistent with that described by the immortality of the soul view.

It can be argued on the basis of the many scriptural passages given in the statement of the Biblical materialist view that neither the soul view nor its companion, the doctrine of the immortality of the soul, is Biblical. This argument rests squarely on the contention that "in the Old Testament it (the soul) never means the immortal soul, but is essentially the life principle, or the living being."[29] In the New Testament there is only one clear reference to 'spirit' which can be taken to mean an independent substantial immaterial being, consistent with the way the soul is defined in the soul view. This reference is in the Gospel of John: "God is spirit, and those who worship him must worship in spirit and truth" (John 4:24).

The concept of immortality itself is "relatively rare in biblical thought, occurring only in Rom. 2:7, I Cor. 15:53-54, I Tim. 6:16, and II Timothy 1:10."[30] In none of these instances is there the slightest suggestion of the view that I have been calling the immortality of the soul view with its philosophical basis in the dualistic soul view. It may, therefore, be concluded that the doctrine of the immortality of the soul is not Biblical. On the basis of philosophical criticisms leveled above it may also be concluded that this view is not philosophically plausible.

The doctrine of the resurrection of the dead is the theory of life after death which is companion to what I called the Biblical materialist view. According to this doctrine man is born. In his freedom he chooses other than what God has called him to do and be. Thus is his sin. The wages of sin are death. Man dies. He breathes his last, as all that which animates him is exhaled. His blood dries up. Man is dead, really dead. God resurrects from the dead those who are faithful. This resurrection or spiritual body is a transformation of the whole person. It is a new creation.

The resurrection doctrine speaks of the resurrection of the dead. Earlier it was stressed that Jesus really died. It was finished. It is necessary to stress the genuine death, not only to show the full humanity of Jesus, but also to show God's new creation. "If life is to issue out of so genuine a death as this, a new divine act of creation is necessary."[31] This is what the Bible proclaims, that in him we are a "new creation," "the whole man, who has really died, is recalled to life by a new act of creation by God. Something has happened—a miracle of creation."[32] There is a new creation, a whole new creation of the whole man. "This is a new creation of matter, an incorruptible matter."[33] The Biblical Christian's hope concerns not only man's individual fate. There is another new creation, which in II Peter is called no less than "new heavens and a new earth" (II Peter 3:13).

It may now be argued that this doctrine of the resurrection of the dead, unlike the doctrine of the immortality of the soul, is philosophically plausible. I will argue this point by showing that the resurrection doctrine can meet each of the four difficulties attributed to the immortality doctrine. What difficulties it does have are relatively minor.

The first problem was that of personal identity, the problem of seeing how the person surviving death is the same person who died. If at or sometime after death there is a resurrection of the body, then the personal identity of the survivor can be justified by recognition of his body. No reference need be made to a soul or spiritual entity, which is unobservable in principle.

In the New Testament Jesus appeared to his disciples after the resurrection. The resurrection body is perceivable and locatable at a certain point in space. In the Biblical account Thomas did not actually touch Jesus as is often supposed. Jesus appeared to the disciples, including Thomas, saying to him, "Put your finger here, and see my hands; and put out your hand, and place it in my side" (John 20:27). Immediately after these words of Jesus the Bible simply says "Thomas answered him, 'My Lord and my God!' " (John 20:28). We may infer from this famous scene, I think, only that Jesus was touchable, not that he was touched. It is also clear that the disciples could see that the resurrection body, which was appearing to them was the same person, Jesus of Nazareth, who had been known to them prior to death.

That there is this resurrection or spiritual body also allows us to see how our second problem, the problem of individuation, may be solved. Where it is impossible to individuate between disembodied souls, it may be seen that the process of individuation is clearly conceivable between resurrection bodies. Fundamentally we individuate people after death by their appearances to us, just as is done in this life.

The third problem was that it was not the whole person who survived. This clearly is not the case in the resurrection doctrine. In ordinary life a man is body infused with life, an animated body. That life may be seen to be the spirit of God. But this is precisely how the life of the spiritual or resurrection body is to be understood. It is a body transformed and made alive by the spirit of God. What survives death is not simply a spiritual remnant of the person.

The fourth difficulty was in the very concept of a disembodied surviving life, which would have to be explicated by the proponents of the immortality doctrine. To be sure the resurrection body, having been transformed, is a spiritual and not a physical body; it still remains a body, however, which appears in space. Such appearance is in clear contrast to the disembodied soul, which does not appear by definition. It is true, although trivially so, that a body which appears can appear to perceive, hear, touch and act as well as move. There is a clear sense, therefore, in which in the resurrection doctrine there is not the problem of the kind of life had by a disembodied existence in the after life.

Perhaps, in the answers to these problems in the philosophy of mind which the resurrection doctrine is able to meet, I have been too sanguine about the concept of the resurrection body itself. What is it to be resurrection body? In the *locus classicus* for the resurrection of Christ in I Corinthians Chapter 15, Paul affirms the resurrection, but he does not tell precisely what the resurrection body is. This body is "imperishable" (vs. 42), "raised in power" (vs. 43). It is raised "a spiritual body" (vs. 44), which follows the physical. Persons are "changed" (vs. 52). Our mortal natures "put on immortality" (vs. 53).

Reference is often made to the resurrection body being a transformed body. Presumably this means that the physical body of ordinary life, with physical properties of weight, mass, shape, etc., are transformed so that the body has the appearance of the physical body but not the physical properties themselves. What appears or the spiritual body itself is the spirit of God which is the transforming power.

As was evident in the discussion of the resurrection this transformed body is odd. It can go through doors that are closed as the resurrected Jesus did, yet it can be touched as Jesus invited Thomas to do. In Luke Chapter 24 after the resurrection Jesus talks to his disciples, even though they did not recognize him (vss. 15-16), while he was walking with them along the road to Emmaus. He supped with them, eating bread and in the doing of this act making himself recognizable (vs. 30), "vanished out of their sight" (vs. 31), only to reappear again to the disciples in Jerusalem (vs. 36). In an effort to comfort them the resurrected Jesus said, "See my hands and my feet, that it is I myself; handle me, and see; for a spirit has not flesh and bones as you see that I have" (vss. 39-40). To prove his point, "while they still disbelieved for joy" he took some fish and "ate before them" (vss. 41 and 43).

The usual similes explaining the resurrection are useful only to a point. From a caterpillar in a cocoon emerges the butterfly. From a seed of corn comes the ear that grows out of it. An error with all these similes is that the former life is not recognizable in the latter. The resurrected Jesus following the resurrection can be recognized, even if there are incidents when he is not so recognized. In spite of this recognizability, however, there is a residual problem, which is to understand clearly, without resort to misleading similes, the resurrection body and how it is related to the physical.

It does not help much to talk here of a transformation of the body, presumably from a physical body to a spiritual body. According to the resurrection of the dead doctrine, the whole self, the animated body, is resurrected and in the resurrection the body itself is transformed. It becomes a spiritual or resurrection body. It is difficult to say exactly what this means. Searching I Corinthians Chapter 15 with care brings no enlightenment on this issue. Yet there are questions. Does the resurrection body take up space? It appears to do so, but it is not space in the ordinary sense. When the resurrected Jesus was passing through the doors or walking into the room where his disciples were located there was a span of time when he was in the same space as the physical door or wall.

The fundamental point which makes the resurrection doctrine Biblical and which leaves the residual philosophical problem is that the resurrection or spiritual transformation is a new creation. It is an absolutely new thing created by God. It is, to be sure, a transformation of the old, but it is a new creation following death. It is precisely this element of newness that puts a barrier before the philosophical attempt to understand the resurrection body itself.

I have shown that the resurrection doctrine, with the exception of some unanswered questions concerning the nature of the resurrection body, is philosophically plausible and Biblical. According to this doctrine man is understood to be a figure totally within history. He lives in history, changes in history and dies in history. He is totally subjected to historical processes over which, it is believed, God has dominion.

E. The Historicity of the World

To speak of the historicity of the world implies, as it did in the case of man, that there is nothing in or of the world which is ahistorical, that is, which is not itself subject to historical change. There is nothing that would correspond by analogy to a soul in man understood either as implicitly immortal or eternal. There is nothing about the world which is known outside one's sacred historical relation to God. The world is the sum total of conditions, a stage I called it above, requisite for acknowledging God in Christ as Lord.

Interestingly, the claim about the historicity of the world is at the heart of "the argument from contingency." Richard Taylor, in reformulating this argument, defines the principle of sufficient reasons as "the belief . . . that there is some explanation for the existence of anything whatever, some reason why it should exist rather than not."[34] The world exists. There must, therefore, be some sufficient reason for the existence of the world. This sufficient reason must be found either in the world itself or outside it. "Now if we suppose that the world—i.e., the totality of all things except God—contains within itself the reason for its existence, we are supposing that it exists by its very nature, that is, that it is a necessary being. In that case there would, of course, be no reason for saying that it must depend upon God or anything else for its existence . . . . This, however, is implausible, for we find nothing about the world or anything in it to suggest that it exists by its own nature."[35] The argument concludes that God, who is both "self-caused" and a "necessary being" is that upon which the world depends.

My particular interest here is in explaining and defending the view that the world is historical to its roots. So far, that means the claim that there is nothing in the world which makes it a necessary being and, therefore, sufficient unto itself. If there were such a thing in or of the world which existed by its own nature, that would necessarily be both eternal and indestructible. "Nothing about the world seems at all like this, for concerning anything in the world, we can perfectly easily think of it as being annihilated, or as never having existed in the first place, without there being the slightest hint of any absurdity in such a supposition."[36] Thus is the historicity of the world.

Is there any reason to disagree with Taylor's conclusion? It may be said that while it is true of anything in the world that may be thought of as being annihilated, such a thought may not be entertained about "matter," defined as that of which anything in the world is composed. The question is, therefore, what knowledge does man possess of "matter," so defined.

Within man's sacred history what he knows is what appears to him. Its origin is beyond his understanding. As we saw above, that is what the creativity of God comes to. So man's knowledge of his "world" is restricted to what appears to man, that is, to what can be experienced. Physical theorists might posit some stuff underlying that which appears. They may formulate the conception of "matter," and they might and do define it as that of which anything is composed or made. They might ascribe certain attributes to this underlying stuff, such as eternality and indestructibility. The concept of matter as so defined would in a sense be parallel to the conception of traditional theologians of God as eternal and therefore indestructible.

I showed that according to the historicist perspective man has no knowledge of the eternality of God. A parallel conclusion can here be drawn with respect to matter. Insofar as man's knowledge is restricted to appearances in his "world," he has no knowledge of "matter," which by definition is that stuff underlying and undergirding those things which are experienced. What man knows is restricted to his sacred historical relation to God and to the world of appearances God has created for him.

If the principle of sufficient reason in the argument from contingency correctly applies to the world, then it may be concluded that the world does depend on God, for the world is not a sufficient reason for its own existence. If this may be concluded should it not also be argued that the argument from contingency is valid?

I wish to argue that the argument from contingency is not valid. It is not a necessary truth, given the premises of the argument, that the world depends on God. Indeed this conclusion is in accord with what man knows in his sacred historical relation with God. Man has no necessary knowledge that there is matter, as I have already argued. It also is the case, however, that man has no necessary knowledge that matter does not exist. If matter does exist then the conclusion of the argument from contingency is fallacious. According to the historicist perspective such a conclusion is something outside the bounds of what man knows.

In the argument from contingency it is concluded that, since there is nothing self-sufficient in and of the world, then the world depends on God. This is to claim that God created the world, and the world itself, unlike God, is not a necessary being. Again such a conclusion accords with the historicist perspective but this does not mean the conclusion of the argument from contingency is valid. That there may not be an ultimate dependence on a creator follows from the possibility of an infinite regress of causes and effects. Each event in the world may be understood to be the effect of a cause(s) which in turn may be the effect of cause(s) *ad infinitum*. According to the historicist perspective there is no knowledge that this is not the case. In the argument from contingency there is nothing to rule out this possibility. Unless and until such knowledge or the ruling out of such a possibility is forthcoming, the argument from contingency can not legitimately be termed "valid."

F. Solutions to Theological and Philosophical Problems
(1) The Problem of Spiritual and Moral Autonomy

The brief statement of the problem of spiritual and moral autonomy is this: If God, who gave man his spiritual and moral autonomy, is to be one's Lord, then one has to sacrifice the very autonomy given by God. This statement of the problem requires revision. It needs to be said that man has to be willing that his spiritual and moral autonomy be sacrificed. This is a preferable statement, for it implies that sacrificing autonomy is not something man does or can do as a free autonomous agent. Man's autonomy is one of the conditions of his existence as a moral and spiritual being. If man's autonomy is to be sacrificed he has to undergo a change in the conditions of his existence, and such a change from an autonomous being is not something man does or can do as a free autonomous agent. Man's autonomy has to be sacrificed by another power in spite of and in conflict with his desires for his own autonomy.

If man is willing that his spiritual and moral autonomy be sacrificed, what he is to do is to let go in the sense of surrendering himself, and concentrating on God, that power to which he has surrendered himself. In the language of the garden he has to let his consciousness be dominated by a consciousness of God. In the language of Matthew he is to seek first the kingdom of God and his righteousness. In the language of personal maturity he becomes entirely self-insufficient. He lets himself go, being willing that the autonomous condition of his life be changed, being willing that he be driven by the power of God and moved by the will of God in him. His own autonomous will power which drives and moves him normally has been sacrificed.

In this power the Biblical Christian becomes a new person, still retaining his individuality, but being new in the sense that the object of his consciousness and the voluntary power which moves and drives him is no longer his, but is God's. Paradoxically, he will have a new sense of moral and spiritual autonomy, which is not his to nourish as did the woman in the garden, but rather which is a gift of God who is Lord of his history. His new individuality simply is the expression of the gifts of the Holy Spirit being worked out in and through him.

Consider at this point the superficially odd question as to whether one becomes a Christian and then grows as a Christian or whether one is always trying to be a Christian and grows up to that point. A parallel question may be asked for the mature person. The answer to the problem of spiritual and moral autonomy suggests that in a sense one is always trying to be a Christian. In the sacred historical story everything is put into the process of becoming a Christian. One is always trying to achieve what one cannot achieve, because it is given as a gift. But the gift given is an achievement, albeit not ours. It is something that happens most often in spite of one's own spiritual and moral autonomous selves. It is a process the result of which is not a free voluntary act of an autonomous self. If one grows one grows in the sense that it is more likely to happen. When it happens, then in a strong sense a person is a Biblical Christian.

In the rehearsal of sacred historical story we saw a culmination in the moment of Jesus the Christ in which one becomes a Biblical Christian. In Section 9 we discussed growth in the maturity of Christ. From the new beginning when we are again taken possession of by the Holy Spirit at Pentecost there are certain spiritual dynamics in us. We are Biblical Christians in a newly created fellowship we call the Church. We live under the enabling grace of God in the fivefold movement of remembrance, expectation, waiting, working and hoping.

The growth in maturity occurs during the interim moment between the inauguration of the kingdom in Christ and its final establishment in the end of sacred history. There is a sense, however, that in this end there is in Biblical Christians a final establishment of the new conditions of our lives—that the object of our consciousness and the voluntary power which moves us is God. The end is unbroken communion with God. In the end this still is what it is to become a Biblical Christian.

(2) The Problem of Freedom

Within the rehearsal of the sacred historical story so far it is clear that man as created by God is free in the sense that he may choose, may determine for himself, to do something other than what God calls him to do and be. To reject this freedom is to choose to be faithful. In the language of maturity in the rehearsal it has been to choose to be dependent, even self-insufficient. In Biblical Christian language it is to choose to be bound to God's call for one's life. In the language of the problem of spiritual and moral autonomy it is to let one's autonomy go. The consequences of these choices is nothing less than the loss of freedom, independence and self-sufficiency. As a Biblical Christian, who takes God in Christ as Lord, one is unfree.

This position may be developed by reference to the concepts of foreknowledge, predestination, determinism, fatalism and indeterminism. If God calls man to do certain specific acts, to have certain specific traits, then he must know prior to man's actual choices either what man will do and be or at least what the options are for man. If the Biblical Christian has the freedom to be unfaithful to God's call then God does not know the actual choice or actions which will be made or done. If he did know these actual choices then there would not be the freedom in man to be unfaithful. What God foreknows is determined for knowledge implies the truth of what is known. If it were otherwise God would not know what he knows. To protect the sense of freedom I want I will define 'foreknowledge' as follows: God knows prior to man's actual choices what the options are for man to choose. He does not know what man actually will choose or will do. To say that God predestines man will, accordingly, mean that God predestines that all men will surrender allegiance to themselves and let God in Christ be their Lord. It also means, however, that he allows man the freedom to be unfaithful to what he predestines.

The Biblical Christian knows the predestination of God in terms of grace. In knowing God's grace man has no power to resist that grace, for in his loss of autonomy he has chosen to let that power be sacrificed. He has, in general, lost the power of the self usually associated with will power, which gives man the power to act. Insofar as the Biblical Christian takes God in Christ as Lord the power which moves man to act is not in or of man himself.

Thus there is a sense in which God determines the acts and the traits of the Biblical Christian whose autonomy has been sacrificed. Generally, determinism is the view that every event is the necessary effect of some cause. According to the historicist perspective all the choices of the Biblical Christian are the necessary effects of God's causal power, i.e., the power of God's grace which impels man to act and which man has not the power to resist. Insofar as the Biblical Christian has lost this power there is no freedom in him.

This is not entirely to espouse a fatalism. Fatalism may be defined as the view that determinism is true with the addition of the belief that the cause of human action is entirely outside one's control. In a sense, of course, for the Biblical Christian the cause of his action, God's grace, is outside his control, but in a sense it is not. The Biblical Christian may be fatalistically determined insofar as he is faithful, but not so if he is unfaithful. The faithful Biblical Christian has, as I have argued, the freedom not to be a Biblical Christian, i.e., to choose to do and be something other than what God calls on him to do and be.

Indeterminism is the view which entails the denial of determinism. This is to believe that it is not the case that every event is the necessary effect of some cause. There are strong and weak senses of this indeterministic thesis. The strong sense is the view that everything happens at random. The weak sense is that some things happen at random and some things do not. According to the historicist perspective both of these senses of indeterminism are to be rejected, for whatever man does happens as a result of some cause or other: the cause of God for the Biblical Christian or the cause of man's self-determination if man is unfaithful.

(3) The Problem of Evil

At the outset the problem may be stated in the form of questions as follows: Do the innocent really suffer; do the wicked prosper? If so, what of the doctrine of moral retribution in this life, and the almost categorical promises of the Deuteronomic law that the righteous will prosper and the wicked will perish?

Even a casual look at the rehearsal of the sacred historical story will provide the following sorts of general answers. The innocent faithful do suffer, and there will be times in which they are envious of the arrogant when they see the prosperity of the wicked (Psalms 73:3). There will be for the faithful, for the innocent, these times of torturing doubt, until they realize that "nevertheless" God is still present. When the Biblical Christian knows God in Christ as Lord there is an inward transformation in the presence of God.

Throughout the rehearsal of the moments of the sacred historical story it was clear that being faithful does not mean that one would not experience or that one would not have to endure times of temptation, or times of trial and emotional confusion. It was clear how the Bible is quite specific and realistic about human problems, even about the suffering of the innocent and the faithful, even about times when there does not seem to be just distribution of rewards and punishments among men. The Deuteronomic success formula, on one level, is much too simplistic, for the life of the faithful is not one of continued unabated prosperity. There are even fall of Jerusalem moments of despair and the loss of hope, compounded by exile moments, in which one is still hopeless and in which one cannot see how or when this hope can be revived, moments when nevertheless one can say as did Isaiah: "Every valley shall be lifted up, and every mountain and hill be made low; . . . And the glory of the Lord shall be revealed" (Isaiah 40:4-5).

But the lessons of the rehearsal include the view that God is still present preparing the Biblical Christian to receive his Lordship. No matter how he feels, God is with the one who is faithful, but who nevertheless suffers. Little does he know it, as Isaiah points out, but God also is with the others. The point of the fact that man suffers does not mean that God is not with him. But, of course, in the moments of anguish, man does not know this, as he may, like the Psalmist in Psalm 73, be full of torturing self-doubt. He can say that it is a wearisome task to understand these things, or even that he cannot understand these things and the trying is wearisome, until he enters into the presence and knowledge of God. Then it is that he sees that "nevertheless" that in spite of all his problems God is still with him, and there is still hope no matter what (see Psalm 73:16-26).

Another most stubborn aspect of the problem is indicated by the question of the origin of evil, often stated as follows: "From whence cometh evil?" A return to the discussion of the moment in the garden after the fall would be a convenient way to get at the problem of the origin of evil. There was found in that beginning moment the story of the woman in the garden and the serpent in Genesis Chapter 3. I said that the serpent himself was not bad, for it was part of God's good creation. The acts of the serpent in either quoting or contradicting God were not bad or evil in themselves. What was evil originated in the exercise of the capacity for free choice, which the woman did make, to succumb to the temptation to be like God herself, knowing good and evil for her own life. The evil lies in the exercise of capacity to choose freely that man will be his own lord. The evil lies in the consequences which follow from making such a choice, for as it was said at the moment in the garden, the choice of the woman created the problem for which the rest of the Bible was the answer. The suffering of the innocent is a consequence of his wrestling, consciously or unconsciously, with this fundamental choice. The innocent are people who are free to choose to be faithful. In this sense, at least, all men are innocent. All men are not innocent in the sense that they all have and do always choose to be faithful. In this sense no men are innocent. These lessons are clear in the rehearsal.

So far I have argued that being a Biblical Christian does not mean that one will not suffer or be in pain or anguish. Secondly, I have argued that evil is rather a function of man's free choice to be unfaithful.

A distinction may be drawn between two types of evil, which often are called "moral evil" and "natural evil." I will define these terms as follows: "Moral evil" refers to suffering, pain or anguish caused by someone doing something immoral or wrong. "Natural evil" on the other hand, is suffering, pain and anguish caused by natural forces or events, i.e., those other than immoral acts. Clearly there is a solution to the problem of moral evil proposed in the above. Moral evil results from man's free choice to be unfaithful, that is, to do something which for the Biblical Christian is wrong.

What position can be taken on the problem of natural evil? According to my perspective there is no natural evil. If there are instances in the Biblical story in which suffering, pain or anguish is caused by natural forces or events, then these forces or events are themselves signs of God's presence in the world. And God's acts, which we moderns call natural events, are done in response to the free choice of man to choose to be unfaithful to God's call for him. They are in this sense a form of punishment for unfaithfulness; or they set the stage of the world in such a way that man will see the error of his ways.

Notice one sharp and important implication of this view of evil according to the historicist perspective. Strictly speaking, evil does not exist. To say that evil lies in the capacity, a God-given capacity which man has, to make free choices, implies that prior to the making of these free choices evil is not an existent thing or person or devil or Satan. Evil may be seen not as an existent thing, but as a lack or a privation of or from what is good. Evil results from a lack of the exercising of man's capacity to choose to be faithful and to let oneself go. Repeatedly in the rehearsal the consequences of the wrestling with the possibility of making choices for God in Christ was apparent. The claim here is that evil lies in man's capacity to make the wrong choice and in the consequence either of wrestling with it or of succumbing to it. Otherwise there is not evil. This lesson rests firmly on the foundation of the rehearsal of the sacred historical story.

One may object to the position that evil does not exist on the basis of scripture by giving several scriptural passages which seem to commit the Biblical Christian to the existence of evil or Satan. Some selected examples of such passages are as follows. In Luke Chapter 10 it says, "I saw Satan fall like lightning from heaven" (Luke 10:18). In the prologue to the Gospel of John it states that the darkness has not overcome the light (see John 1:5). There are several references in Paul, in which Paul writes of "principalities," which are in creation (see Romans 8:38). This point is emphasized in Colossians, to wit: "For in him all things were created, in heaven and on earth, visible and invisible, whether thrones or dominions or principalities or authorities" (Colossians 1:16). An especially important passage in this connection is in Ephesians, and I quote it as follows: "Put on the whole armor of God, that you may be able to stand against the wiles of the devil. For we are not contending against flesh and blood, but against the principalities, against the powers, against the world rulers of this present darkness, against the spiritual hosts of wickedness in the heavenly places" (Ephesians 6:11-12). A final passage to be selected is in Revelation. Here Michael is referred to. He is fighting against the dragon and his angels. They were defeated. Dragon, "that ancient serpent," was called "the Devil and Satan." He was the "deceiver of the whole world" (Revelation 12:7-9).

Do these or similar passages in the New Testament rule out my position, that, strictly speaking, evil does not exist? To be sure Satan is referred to, and he is called the "ruler of this world." What is the nature of this Satan that supposedly exists? From these passages there would seem to be three interpretations. First, in John, darkness is evil. What is darkness, however, but the absence of light, just as evil may be seen not as something existent, but as a lack of the good?

Secondly, in Revelation Dragon is the evil one, who appears to be identified with the ancient serpent. This may be taken to refer back to the serpent in Genesis Chapter 3. I have, however, already argued that it was not the serpent that was evil. Rather the evil lay in man's capacity to want to be a little god knowing good and evil for himself.

As to who is Satan, who supposedly exists, the major burden of these passages, expecially from Paul, is on thrones, dominions, principalities, authorities and powers. In the passage from Ephesians, Paul says man is not "against flesh and blood," rather against these principalities and powers.

These indeed are in creation as is stated in Romans (see Romans 8:38). But what is it that one is committing oneself to when one commits himself to the existence of such as these? For an indication of the problems in this question consider the following entry under "Principality" in the *Interpreter's Dictionary of the Bible*: "A term used in the plural form . . . referring to the organized cosmological powers of angels in Rom. 8:38 (see Angel). As the connection with the specifically named 'angels' shows, a 'principality' is thought of as an extra group of spirits which may interfere with and hinder the salvation of Christ. The underlying pattern is mythological and not entirely clear. For similar lists see Ephesians 1:21, and Col. 1:16. Paul's idea is obvious: No power in the world can destroy God's love; it is greater than and superior to all demonic forces."[37] According to the historicist perspective it is "powers in the world," which are the only powers there are, which man freely chooses to follow and by so choosing to deny the Lordship of God in Christ. According to Paul these powers are principalities, or powers, or thrones or dominions or authorities. It may not be "entirely clear" what it is to identify these realities with demonic spirits which seek to destroy God's love. It is even less clear how these realities may be identified with an individual evil force or personification in the devil or Satan. It seems more plausible to identify such realities as these with the results of man's systematic decisions to choose something other than God in Christ as Lord of his life. Such free choices are the soil in which principalities and powers grow.

(4) Universalism and the Problem of "The Others"

Within the historicist perspective the line of the solution to the problem of "the others" is this. God makes available to all the fruits of his promises. In the discussion of the problem of freedom I defined the concept of predestination, holding this to be the view that God predestines that all should be saved but that he allows them to choose to do and be otherwise. This version of God's wishes towards all men comes out clearly in II Peter, to wit: "The Lord is not slow about his promises as some count slowness, but is forbearing towards you, not wishing that any should perish, but that all should reach repentance" (II Peter 3:9). Nevertheless, as is amply evident, some people choose freely not to do or be what God has called them to do or be.

From what has been given it does not follow that all will be saved. Universalism is not true as it has been defined. God has made available his promises to all. Some have chosen and continue to choose otherwise. These people are the stubbornly unrepentant. There clearly are degrees of unrepentance here, for some choose otherwise occasionally and some systematically and regularly and intentionally choose otherwise. There are others who simply do not care, but by their uncaring attitude reflect a free negative choice.

As we saw in the rehearsal the class of persons called "the others" clearly is a mixed lot. Consider sub-class (4), those sincere believers and practitioners of religious traditions other than Christianity. This group adds additional complications to the problem. If the moments in the sacred historical story could be translated into moments in the religious life of exponents of other religious traditions then people in this sub-class are not to be classed among the "others." The possibility of such translations is another long story, not to be attempted here.

The view taken on the problem of "the others" will be determined to some extent on the view taken about the fact that the kingdom of God has not yet come. In the rehearsal, in Section 9, three beliefs were proposed for the Biblical Christian. If he takes the first alternative, that the kingdom of God still is near at hand and that people had best be getting ready, then his sense of anticipation will be heightened and also his sense of judgment. All the problems that there are in the world will be painfully evident. If the end is to come soon there will be widespread and harsh judgment.

If, however, he takes the second alternative, that the kingdom of God is a present possession, then his sense of anticipation will be weakened, and so also his sense of judgment. The Gospel of John might well be followed at this point. It would be said that people who hear and believe have eternal life now as a present possession. Those who do not hear and do not believe do not have, but they could have it if they did so hear and believe.

Biblical Christians might naturally work to the end that "the others" might hear and believe. Since, however, eternal life is regarded as a present possession, man does not look forward to a time when those who have it will be saved and those who do not have it will be judged and rejected.

If he takes the third alternative, that the end is farther off than he had once supposed, then he might well follow the line taken up by II Peter. Accordingly, the Lord wishes that "all should reach repentance." He does not wish that any should perish. Since he is forebearing towards all, and since he wishes the repentance of all mankind, and yet again since he gives all their freedom it seems as if the end is and will continue to be far off. But "with the Lord one day is as a thousand years, and a thousand years as one day" (II Peter 3:8). The Biblical Christian would also wish that all should reach repentance, that not any should perish. They might well work to this end, that any that come within their spheres of influence should themselves hear and believe. It must be remembered, of course, that the other always has a negative freedom.

But according to this third alternative, there is an end, a judgment in the future. The day of the Lord will come, the earth as it is known will be destroyed, and there will be a judgment. Such a moment will be at that time, at the time of a final or last judgment, that those who have not heard and believed will be lost, that those who continue to make the free negative choices will be counted among "the others."

11

Footnotes

Section 1

[1]The Bible, Revised Standard Version (New York: Thomas Nelson and Sons, New Testament, 1946; Old Testament, 1952). Note: All references from the Bible will be taken from the Revised Standard Version.

[2]Horace English and Ava Champney, *A Comprehensive Dictionary of Psychological and Psycholoanalytic Terms* (New York: Longman's Green and Co., 1958), p. 308.

[3]English and Champney, p. 308.

Section 2

[1]H.G. May and Bruce M. Metzger, eds., *The New Oxford Annotated Bible,* Revised Standard Version (New York: Oxford University Press, 1973), pp. 1-4.

[2]Barbara Schodt, from a term paper in Religious Studies 250, Themes in Biblical Literature, Longwood College, 1977.

Section 4

[1]Herbert Bronstein, ed., *A Passover Haggadah*, rev. ed. (New York: Penguin Books, 1978), p. 29.

Section 6

[1]John B. Hayes, *Introduction to the Bible* (Philadelphia: The Westminster Press, 1969), p. 112.

[2]George A. Buttrick, ed., *Interpreter's Bible* (Nashville: Abingdon Press, 1962), Vol. 2, p. 1100.

[3]Bernard Anderson, *Understanding the Old Testament,* 3rd ed. (Englewood Cliffs, New Jersey: Prentice Hall, 1975), pp. 297-298.

[4]Anderson, pp. 298-299.

[5]Hayes, p. 201.

[6]Hayes, p. 203.

[7]Hayes, pp. 203-204.

Section 7

[1]Anderson, p. 450.

[2]Anderson, p. 454.

[3]Anderson, pp. 459-462.

[4]Anderson, p. 472, from Pritchard, *Ancient and Near Eastern Texts*, p. 316.

[5]Anderson, pp. 497-498.

Section 8

[1]Hayes, p. 320; quoted from *Vita Claudii*, xxv.5.

[2]Hayes, p. 320; quoted from *Annales*, xv. 44.

[3]Norman Perrin, *The New Testament* (New York: Harcourt, Brace and Janovich, Inc., 1974), p. 283.

[4]Perrin, p. 283.

[5]Hayes, pp. 320-321; quoted from *Antiquities,* xviii.33.

[6]Perrin, pp. 283-284.

[7]Perrin, p. 285.

[8]Perrin, p. 285.

[9]Hayes, p. 323.

[10]Perrin, p. 279.

[11]H. C. Kee, F. W. Young, and F. Froelich, *Understanding the New Testament*, 3rd ed. (Englewood, New Jersey: Prentice Hall, 1973), pp. 81-82.

[12]Perrin, p. 279.

[13]Perrin, pp. 281-282.

[14]Gustaf Aulen, *Jesus in Contemporary Historical Research*, trans. Ingalill H. Hjelm (Philadelphia: Fortress Press, 1973), p. 3.

[15]Michael Grant, *Jesus* (New York: Charles Scribner's Sons, 1977), p. 10.

[16]Aulen, p. 1.

[17]Aulen, p. 10.

[18]Aulen, p. 30.

[19]Aulen, p. 10.

[20]Aulen, p. 202.

[21]George Buttrick, ed. *Interpreter's Dictionary of the Bible* (Nashville: Abingdon Press, 1962), Vol. 4, p. 414.

[22]Buttrick, *Interpreter's Dictionary*, vol. 4, pp. 414-415.

[23]Oscar Cullman, "Immortality of the Soul or Resurrection of the Dead," in *Immortality*, ed. Terrence Penelhum (Belmont, Ca.: Wadsworth Publishing Co., 1973), p. 61.

[24]Cullmann, pp. 61-62.

[25]Cullmann, p. 63.

[26]Gordon Kaufman, *Systematic Theology: A Historicist Perspective* (New York: Charles Scribner's Sons, 1968), p. 413.

[27]Kaufman, p. 414.

[28]Kaufman, p. 420, nt. 17.

Section 9

[1]Gustaf Aulen, *The Faith of the Christian Church*, trans. Eric H. Walstrom (Philadelphia: Fortress Press, 1960), p. 292.

[2]Hans Kung, *The Church* (New York: Image Books, Doubleday and Co., 1976), p. 105.

[3]Kung, p. 105.

[4]Kung, p. 106.

[5]Kung, p. 108

[6]Kung, p. 109

[7]The New Oxford Annotated Bible, p. 1364. (See also Romans 7:7 and Galatians 3:19-29, including the OAB commentary on these passages.)

[8]Buttrick, *Interpreter's Dictionary*, vol. 3, p. 21.

[9]Grant, p. 10.

[10]Grant, pp. 10-11

[11]Buttrick, *Interpreter's Dictionary*, vol. 3, p. 21.

[12]Perrin, p. 201

[13]Buttrick, *Interpreter's Dictionary*, vol. 4., p. 261.

Section 10

[1]Paul Edwards, ed., *The Encyclopedia of Philosophy* (New York: MacMillan Publishing Co., 1967), vol. 4, p. 24.

[2]Edwards, p. 24.

[3]Keith E. Yandell, ed., *God, Man and Religion* (New York: McGraw Hill Book Co., 1973), p. 185

[4]Yandell, p. 185.

[5]Edwards, vol. 5, p. 301.

[6]Edwards, p. 302.

[7]Kaufman, p. xv.

[8]Kaufman, p. xv.

[9]Dom Cyprian Vagaggini, *Theological Dimensions of the Liturgy* (Collegeville, Minn.: The Liturgical Press, 1976).

[10]John Hick, *Philosophy of Religion*, 3rd ed. (Englewood Cliffs, N.J.: Prentice Hall, 1973), pp. 5-14.

[11]Hick, p. 8.

[12]Hick, p. 8.

[13]Hick, p. 9.

[14]Hick, p. 11.

[15]Hick, p. 12.

[16]Hick, p. 14.

[17]Kaufman, p. 14.

[18]Kaufman, p. 14.

[19]Kaufman, p. 329.

[20]Levi A. Olan, *Judaism and Immortality* (New York: Union of Maerican Hebrew Congregations, 1971), p. 9.

[21]Olan, p. 9.

[22]Olan, p. 9.

[23]Terrence Penelhum, *Survival and Disembodied Existence* (New York: Humanities Press, 1970), pp. 76-77.

[24]David Hume, *A Treatise of Human Nature*, ed. L.A. Selby-Bigge (Oxford: Clarendon Press, 1888), Book I, Part IV, Section VI.

[25]Penelhum, pp. 19-36, 37-44.

[26]Penelhum, p. 35.

[27]Penelhum, p. 35.

[28]Penelhum, p. 42.

[29]Buttrick, *Interpreter's Dictionary*, vol. 4, p. 428.

[30]A. Cohen and H. Halverson, eds., *A Handbook of Christian Theology* (New York: Oxford University Press, 1958), p. 183.

[31]Cullmann, p. 65.

[32]Cullmann, p. 65.

[33]Cullmann, p. 73.

[34]Richard Taylor, in *God, Man and Religion*, ed. Keith E. Yandell (New York: McGraw Hill Book Co., 1973), p. 419.

[35]Taylor, p. 423.

[36]Taylor, p. 423.

[37]Buttrick, *Interpreter's Dictionary*, vol. 3, p. 891.

12

Bibliography

Anderson,Bernard. *Understanding the Old Testament*. 3rd. ed. Englewood Cliffs, N.J.: Prentice Hall, 1975.

Aulen, Gustaf. *Jesus in Contemporary Historical Research*. Trans. Ingalill H. Hjelm. Philadelphia: Fortress Press, 1973.

_____. *The Faith of the Christian Church*. Trans. Eric H. Walstrom. Philadelphia: Fortress Press, 1960.

The Bible. Revised Standard Version. New York: Thomas Nelson and Sons, 1946, 1952.

Bornkamm, Gunther. *Jesus of Nazareth*. Trans. Irene and Fraser McLuskkey. New York: Harper and Row, 1960.

Bruce, F. F. *Jesus and Christian Origins Outside the New Testament*. Grand Rapids, Michigan: William B. Eerdmans Publishing Co., 1974.

Buttrick, George, ed. *Interpreter's Bible*. In Twelve Volumes. Nashville: Abingdon Press, 1962.

_____, ed. *Interpreter's Dictionary of the Bible*. In Five Volumes. Nashville: Abingdon Press, 1962, 1976.

Cahn, Stephen. "The Irrelevance of Proofs to Religious Belief." In *God, Man and Religion*, pp. 498-502. Ed. K. E. Yandell. New York: McGraw Hill, 1973.

Cohen, A. and Halverson, H., eds. *A Handbook of Christian Theology*. New York: World Publishing Co., 1958.

Cross, F. L., ed. *The Oxford Dictionary of the Christian Church*. New York: Oxford University Press, 1958.

Cullmann, Oscar. "Immortality of the Soul or Resurrection of the Dead." In *Immortality*, pp. 53-85. Ed. Terrence Penelhum. Belmont, California: Wadsworth Pub. Co., 1973.

Dodd, C. H. The *Founder of Christianity*. New York: Macmillan Pub. Co., 1970.

_____. The Parables of the Kingdom. New York: Charles Scribner's Sons. 1961.

Edwards, Paul, ed. *The Encyclopedia of Philosophy*. In Eight Volumes. New York: Macmillan Pub. Co., 1967.

English, Horace B. and Champney, Ava. *A Comprehensive Dictionary of Psychological and Psycholoanalytic Terms*. New York: Longman's Green and Co., 1958.

Flew, Anthony and Macintyre, Alasdair, eds. *New Essays in Philosophical Theology*. London: SCM Press, 1955.

Fuller, R. H. *A Critical Introduction to the New Testament*. Longdon: Duckworth, 1966.

Geach, Peter. *God and the Soul*. London: Routledge and Kegan Paul, 1969.

_____. "Immortality." in *Immortality*, pp. 11-21. Ed. Terrence Pennelhum. Belmont, California: Wadsworth Pub. Co., 1973.

Grant, Michael. *Jesus*. New York: Charles Scribner's Sons, 1977.

Harvey, Van A. *A Handbook of Theological Terms*. New York: Macmillan and Co., 1964.

Herbert, R. T. *Paradox and Identity in Theology*. Ithaca, N.Y.: Cornell University Press, 1979.

Hick, John. *Death and Eternal Life*. New York: Harper and Row, 1976.

_____. *Philosophy of Religion*. 3rd ed. Englewood Cliffs, N.J.: Prentice Hall, 1983.

Hume, David. *A Treatise of Human Nature*. Ed. L. A. Selby-Bigge. Oxford: Clarendon Press, 1888.

_____. *Enquiries*. Ed. L. A. Selby-Bigge. Oxford: Clarendon Press, 1888.

_____. *Dialogues Concerning Natural Religion*. New York: Hafner Pub. Co., 1948.

Kaufman, Gordon. *Systematic Theology: A Historicist Perspective*. New York: Charles Scribner's Sons, 1963.

Kee, H. C., Young, F. W., Froelich, F. *Understanding the New Testament*. 3rd ed. Englewood Cliffs N.J.: Prentice Hall, 1973.

Keller, Werner. *The Bible as History*. New York: William Morrow and Co., 1956.

Kierkegaard, Soren. *The Concluding Unscientific Postscript to the Philosophical Fragments*. Trans. David F. Swenson. Princeton: Princeton University Press, 1945.

_____. *Fear and Trembling and Sickness unto Death*. Trans. Walter Lowrie. Princeton University Press, 1941.

_____. *Johannes Climacus*. Trans. T. H. Croxall, Standford, California: Stanford University Press, 1958.

_____. *The Journals of Kierkegaard*. Ed. Alexander Dru. New York: Harper and Row, 1959.

_____. *Purity of Heart*. Trans. Douglas V. Steere. New York: Harper and Row, 1938.

_____. *Philosophical Fragments*. Trans. David F. Swenson. Trans. Revised Howard V. Hong. Princeton: Princeton University Press, 1962.

_____. *Point of View for My Work as an Author*. Trans. Walter F. Lowrie. New York: Harper and Row, 1962.

Kung, Hans. *On Being a Christian*. Trans. Edward Quinn. New York: Doubleday and Co., 1974.

_____. *The Church*. New York: Image Books, Doubleday and Co., 1976.

Lowrie, Walter. *Kierkegaard*. In Two Volumes. New York: Harper and Row, 1962.

Nixon, Robert E. *The Art of Growing*. New York: Random House, 1964.

Olan, Levi A. *Judaism and Immortality*. New York: Union of American Hebrew Congregations, 1971.

Otto, Rudolph. *The Idea of the Holy*. Trans J. W. Harvey. New York: Oxford University Press, 1958.

The New Oxford Annotated Bible. Revised Standard Version. Ed. H. G. May and Bruce M. Metzger. New York: Oxford University Press, 1973.

Penelhum, Terrence, ed. *Immortality*. Belmont, California: Wadsworth Pub. Co., 1973.

_____. *Religion and Rationality*. New York: Random House, 1971.

_____. *Survival and Disembodied Existence*. New York: Humanities Press, 1970.

Perrin, Norman. *The New Testament*. New York: Harcourt, Brace and Janovich, Inc., 1974.

_____. *Rediscovering the Teachings of Jesus*. New York: Harper and Row, 1967.

Plantinga, Alvin, ed. *The Ontological Argument*. New York: Doubleday and Co., 1965.

Purtill, Richard L. *Thinking about Religion*. Englewood Cliffs, N.J.: Prentice Hall, 1978.

Taylor, Richard. *Metaphysics*. 2nd ed. Englewood Cliffs, N.J.: Prentice Hall, 1974.

Torrence, Thomas F. *Space, Time and Resurrection*. Grand Rapids, Michigan: Eerdmans Pub. Co., 1976.

Vagaggini, Dom Cyprian. *Theological Dimensions of the Liturgy*. Collegeville, Minn.: The Liturgical Press, 1976.

Walker, Williston. *A History of the Christian Church*. Revised Edition. New York: Charles Scribner's Sons, 1959.

Yandell, Keith E., ed. *God, Man and Religion*. New York: McGraw Hill Book Company, 1973.

SYMPOSIUM SERIES